The Small Outsider

The Small Outsider

THE STORY OF AN AUTISTIC CHILD

by JOAN MARTIN HUNDLEY

St. Martin's Press New York

Copyright © 1971 by Joan Martin Hundley
All rights reserved. For information, write:
St. Martin's Press, Inc., 175 Fifth Ave., New York, N.Y. 10010
Printed in Hong Kong
Library of Congress Catalog Card Number: 76-185856
First published in the United States of America in 1972

AFFILIATED PUBLISHERS: Macmillan & Company, Limited, London—also at
Bombay, Calcutta, Madras and Melbourne—The Macmillan Company of Canada,
Limited, Toronto

This is a story about a strange little boy written by an untrained observer—his mother. In it I have tried to describe a condition that, until recently, most people didn't know existed. I don't pretend to understand the condition; I know it exists, but I am not sure what it is. I have just written the things I have seen and the things I feel.

J.H.

There was the Door to which I found no Key;
There was the Veil through which I might not see . . .

OMAR KHAYYÁM

ILLUSTRATIONS

I

IT WAS RAINING THE NIGHT LITTLE DAVID WAS BORN. THE TRIP to hospital was an anxious one, with my husband, David, racing our old car through the busy evening traffic. I remember the reflections of the street lights on the glassy road, and the sound of the wiper sliding and thumping as the rain splashed against the windscreen.

"You're supposed to phone the hospital and let them know you're coming," I said, so David skidded to a stop in front of a phone booth, only to discover, after a frantic search for the right coins, that the phone was out of order.

That's the kind of night it was.

To start with, we had left home without my suitcase and had covered about six blocks before I noticed it wasn't in the car.

Our little daughter Ellen sat placidly in her car seat, having already given us her views on the prospect of a new baby. She told us flatly that she didn't want a little brother in the house. She enjoyed being our baby, and she wasn't going to put up with opposition. Her fluffy blonde hair blew about her face as we sped along. She was only twenty months old, and I hated the thought of leaving her for two weeks. We had never been separated before, and I knew she would fret for me.

Because I didn't want to leave my family I had told the

doctor that I preferred to have this baby at home, but he thought it would be most unwise.

Cold and weary, I sat awkwardly in the front seat of the car. I had been in mild labour for a week, and the chill of the night air made me shiver. I fell to thinking about the past nine months and all that had happened during my pregnancy.

I had been anxious to present my husband with a son, but my age worried me. I had been thirty-eight when Ellen was born, aware of the increased likelihood of mongolism in children born to women over that age; yet here I was, forty years old, very tired, and facing another confinement. I had suffered migraine headaches; my arms and legs had become grotesquely swollen. I had felt dizzy, and sometimes short of breath. I was anaemic, too, and there was a tightness in my throat that worried me. To top it all, I had battled through two severe bouts of gastric flu.

Roley, my fifteen-year-old son from a previous marriage, had missed a lot of schooling through kidney trouble that year, and was having difficulty catching up. He and I had been on our own for many years before my second marriage, and he could not get used to sharing me.

There had been financial problems, too. David had been taking university courses for many years—at first full-time, on scholarship—and neither he nor I had had much money when we married. I had supported Roley for years on a stenographer's salary and had not been able to save.

David and I had been unable to find reasonable accommodation for two adults and a boy within easy travelling distance both from David's job at the Probation and Parole Office and from the University of Melbourne where he attended evening classes. In desperation, I pooled what small sums of money we had between us and recklessly, with astonishing lack of business sense, bought a five-year lease on a run-down apartment house in the suburb of South Yarra. Over the years, working flat out all the time, painting and repairing (the floors kept falling through), I steadily lost money, even when all the rooms were let. I still don't see how I did it. It had all looked so promising on paper.

One disadvantage I had was a habit of selecting tenants

who blew up gas bath-heaters. This ran us into terrific expense. Also, we were incapable of evicting tenants who didn't pay their rent.

Not long after we were married, David took on a new job, Supervisor of Classification and Treatment in Victorian Prisons. This meant that he was in effect deputy to the Director of Prisons. It was a big job with heavy responsibilities, and although he already had his B.A. and Diploma of Social Studies he was still at university, working on his last course, for his Diploma in Criminology. We were very happy and very much in love, but we had each taken on a heavy load—he with his job and study, I with an unsuccessful business for which I had no ability.

I felt uneasy for the health of the baby I was carrying, and had a nagging fear that all was not well.

The doctor had turned the baby twice during the sixth month, and I had felt restless and uncomfortable right through the pregnancy. There was something different about this baby. Like me, it seemed lethargic: too weary to get comfortable.

There had been other anxieties. When I was about five months pregnant the Executive Council of Victoria had decided not to commute the death sentence of one Peter Tait, who had been found guilty of murder. The State was in an uproar over the crime. Everywhere I went, in shops, on street corners, people were talking about the hanging. Once when I visited my doctor for the usual check-up he said, "Tell your husband we don't want undisciplined people like Tait walking round in a respectable community. I hope they make a good job of the hanging." The doctor was a great believer in discipline.

I didn't want to talk about it. I was too worried. I was in love with the intelligent man with a deep respect for human life who because of his job would have to help plan the hanging. I knew what a setback this would be to David's hopes for the future. All his plans for developing the co-operation between prison officers and prisoners necessary for the smooth running of the institutions were to be hindered by this retrograde execution. He said nothing about it, but I knew how he felt and I was sick for him.

3

There were legal arguments for and against hanging, public demonstrations against capital punishment, newspaper headlines. David grew more and more tense. At one time I suggested that he should resign. He told me that it would not save the man's life and he could do more good in the long run by seeing it through, no matter what. As a public servant he was not allowed to express any opinion. It was harder to stay in the job than to resign, but he stayed.

And in his cell in Pentridge prison, waiting to be hanged, sat the most despised, miserable man in all Victoria. I thought of Peter Tait and felt pity. This didn't mean that I condoned the crime, only that I didn't want to see more unnecessary misery. I felt pity for the murderer, the murdered, and the family of the murdered person. And I was consumed with anxiety for my husband. I had trouble sleeping, and when I did sleep nightmares clouded my rest. My limbs ached and my head seemed full of fog. My days were threaded together with grey thoughts, thoughts with no purpose. I was so tired that living became a task. I operated as a robot, I no longer lived for myself, I felt like a mechanical shape. I existed as a means of keeping the baby alive, but I couldn't shake off the nagging fear that there was something wrong with this baby. I felt as though I floated in a void and the world was rushing past too quickly for me. Too many things were worrying me, and every time I allowed myself to think I thought of the hanging.

Eventually the Government Psychiatrist pronounced Peter Tait legally insane and there was no hanging. I shall never forget the feeling of relief that swept through our household. . . .

The screech of the car tyres as we turned a corner and the sight of the hospital looming up ahead brought me back to the present.

We left Ellen sitting in her car seat while we hurried up the steps to the office. I told David not to stay with me after he had carried my suitcase up in the lift and placed it beside the empty bed. I wanted him to get Ellen home out of the cold and tucked into her cot.

4

Through the upstairs window I saw them driving away, Ellen's blonde head swaying at the rear window as they turned the corner under a street lamp.

I wondered what was in the injection they had given me soon after I arrived at the hospital. It made me feel so unreal. The past, present, and future were all one, I was living in a dream, in another dimension. My body was there, lying on a high white bed; my mind was somewhere else.

I didn't know how long I had been lying there; time was floating by in a tangle of confusion; and always there was pain. I tried to pretend there was no pain, but I could hide nothing from the huge lamp in the ceiling above me. It stared down relentlessly and saw my discomfort with its harsh bright eye. And under that fierce yellow light my night stretched into long slow mists of agonizing effort, hour after hour of hazy struggle. Angular shadows moved across the high ceiling. Vague white figures like statues glided by and somewhere there was the sound of rubber-soled shoes squelching on a polished floor.

The pain ebbed and flowed and sometimes I lost consciousness. Scenes flashed past my eyes, hurried pictures of yesterday. I saw myself falling from a horse when I was a child. I remembered my first day at school. There was a thunderstorm in a dark cemetery. Lightning flashed and I saw my grandfather's grave. Bombs were falling from the sky and I was lying in a ditch. Gaudy colours streaked across my vision. Then I saw my mother's face. There were tears in her eyes, as there had been when my brother went to the war. Such a long war. . . .

I heard a muffled moan. Was it my voice? I didn't think so. I don't think I made any noise at all. I could call out if I wanted to, but it wouldn't make any difference. Nothing can help when the claws of pain tear. How much longer? The night must end. Morning must come.

As time passed, half delirious, I fell into uneasy speculation. What if I die tonight? What is death? Death is a void, death is freedom from pain. I am such a small creature in the scheme of the universe, surely I am not important enough to feel so much pain. All matter is subject to change, all life subject to death. Life is fleeting. Tonight, alone, I could slip slowly into death and that would be the end of pain. I am giddy with fatigue. Life is imperfect but life is all we have so life is everything. I don't want to die. The pain won't last for ever. If only I could get more air into my lungs. I am suffocating. Gasp, gasp for air, that is the way to stay alive. I need a sip of water but I couldn't swallow it. A few minutes' sleep would be heaven.

After an age, from somewhere, nowhere, I heard the doctor's voice: "Breathe deeply. Don't give up."

There was a long slow burst of pain, then the last struggle and the preciousness of a new life.

"It's a boy," said the doctor.

"His name is David Martin Hundley," I whispered. "Is he all right? Give him to me."

"He's perfect," said the doctor.

"Phone David," I told him.

"It's five in the morning. Do you want me to wake him?"

"He won't be asleep," I said, and held my son in my arms. I was overwhelmed with relief to see that he was all right.

After I had been taken back to the ward I slept. Oh, how I slept! They woke me for breakfast, but I was asleep again before the tray had been cleared away. I didn't wake up fully until the five o'clock feeding time that evening, when they brought David Martin in for me to feed for the first time. Excitedly I examined him.

He was a fairly large baby, 8 pounds 11 ounces, and beautifully formed. His head was a good shape, with a high intelligent forehead. He lay awake with the wisest look on his handsome face, his arms folded in front of him.

When I pointed out that his skin was a strange yellow colour, the sister told me that he was jaundiced. I was not unduly perturbed; I knew that would pass in a few days. Lots of babies are jaundiced at birth.

But when I tried to feed him I sensed something unusual. He was reluctant to turn his head. He seemed slow to catch on. By the time I got him to start sucking, all the other babies had finished feeding and were being taken back to the nursery. I couldn't get through to him what I wanted. I was dumbfounded. I had breast-fed my other two children without the slightest hitch. There was something strange

6

about this baby. My old uneasiness began to return.

I tried to feed him on the other side, but his head remained turned to where it had been to take the first side. He didn't want to change. He refused to move his head even slightly. It seemed that the only way to feed him on this side would be to hold him upside-down.

I was still puzzling over this predicament when the visitors arrived.

David came towards me, smiling self-consciously. The brim of his hat was fluted and hung down over his eyes.

"What ever happened to your hat?" I asked.

"It fell in the washing-machine," he replied without concern. He looked tired, and I think he had absent-mindedly put on the ruined hat through force of habit. He took the baby's hand.

"Well," he said, "I suppose you're feeling pretty pleased with yourself. You've produced the next David Hundley. I've never seen such a wonderful-looking baby. And he already looks as though he's wondering about the world. We've got a brainy one here for sure." He was bursting with pride and delight.

"Do you think he looks all right?" I asked.

"I think he looks terrific."

So I didn't tell David of my worries. What could I have told him, anyway? Only that I thought there was something wrong. I didn't even know how to put it into words; it would have sounded too silly. Besides, I could have been wrong. But I remained sure that I wasn't.

After the visitors left I tried feeding the baby again. This time he turned his head quite easily for the second side, but jibbed when I wanted him to take the first side again. By the time I managed to get him full of milk the other babies were being brought round for their final feed of the evening. I was patient with children and could mostly understand them, but this one had me stumped.

The nurses and the other mothers in the ward were highly amused at the antics I went through to feed him. Though I didn't think it was funny, I joked with them about it because I couldn't think how to explain my predicament to anyone.

When the nurses started taking the babies back to the

nursery for the night I asked the head sister if she could see anything wrong with little David. She told me he was the fittest and heaviest boy in the nursery. She said that being jaundiced could make him lethargic for a day or so, but it was nothing serious.

I asked to see the doctor as soon as possible.

"In the morning, dear," said the sister. "You're tired. Things will look different in the morning." She patted my arm and took David back to the nursery.

I lay back and looked up at the ceiling and tried to understand why I was so uneasy. What did I expect of a baby born at five o'clock that morning? Of course he was lethargic and clumsy. How could I expect him to know how to feed so soon? I didn't even have a proper milk supply yet. Certainly nobody else thought there was anything wrong with him. Why did I? Because I knew there was, that was why. I didn't know what; I only knew there was something lacking, something I couldn't explain.

The noises of the hospital slowly subsided as the patients settled down for the night. In the distance there was the wail of an ambulance siren, then silence. I lay awake for hours. How was I going to tell my husband?

It was the loneliest night of my life.

The doctor called early the next morning and wanted to know what all the fuss was about. I told him there was something wrong with my baby.

"How do you mean?" he asked.

"Well, he's hard to feed," I said, "and he's sort of uncooperative. But mainly I think it's the way he looks. When I look at him he doesn't look back at me the right way. I don't think he knows I'm there. That's all I can tell you."

"Well, it's not much to go on, is it?" he said with a quizzical smile. "As a matter of fact, young David Martin seems to be doing particularly well. You say he's hard to feed, and yet the scales show he is taking quite a good meal each time. Perhaps you're just a little rusty and have forgotten how to feed a baby quickly. You can't expect a baby to do better than David after just twenty-four hours of life. But I'll tell you what. We'll have blood tests taken. Will that satisfy you?"

The test results were all favourable.

"I can find absolutely nothing wrong with this baby," said the doctor.

"Maybe you haven't tested him for the right things," I said.

"Well, what do you want me to test him for?" he asked.

"I don't know," I answered. "I just don't know. Maybe he's got something that nobody knows about."

After that I kept quiet. What else was there to say? I could have talked for ever, and the doctor would have thought I was being ridiculous. But I knew. After all, this was not my first baby; I had two others to compare him with, and I had handled a lot of babies over the years.

The nurses who supplemented David's feeding in the nursery by bottle could detect nothing wrong with him, though they did say that he had a will of his own, unusual for such a young baby. When I bottle-fed him I found it much simpler because I could move the bottle to any angle that suited him. It was only breast-feeding that was difficult.

But each time I handled David I became more convinced that there was something strange about him. After a few days I dreaded having to look at him. I remember each encounter with him as a souvenir of sorrow. Each time I cradled him in my arms I knew he was not complete.

Every feeding time was difficult, but with practice I learned to cope a little better, for although he could suck quite well and sometimes finished before any of the other babies, he had no idea where the food came from and didn't seem to understand what was required of him. He was still slow at changing from one side to the other and I finished up feeding him on alternate sides—one meal on the right and the next meal on the left.

When he was not drinking he lay perfectly still with his arms across his chest, looking placid and unconcerned. Such a handsome little fellow, and so dignified! The nurses had pet names for all the babies in the nursery. There was a Curly Top, a Snooks, a Baby Pie, and a Baby Bunting. My baby was called Mr Hundley, the Judge.

"Your baby stands out from all the others," one of the nurses told me. "He's so mature and intelligent-looking. When the other babies are squirming and yelling their heads

9

B

off he just lies there quietly looking ahead and thinking. He looks as though he's been here before and knows it all."

But to me he looked like a baby who had suffered severe shock. Minute burst blood-vessels streaked the whites of his eyes. The doctor told me they would clear away in a week or so, but six years later they were still there.

During the day I was very busy in the hospital; the mothers were all good talkers and good company, and the time passed quickly enough. But I dreaded the evenings, when all the mothers were fast asleep and the cheerful nurses were off duty. Then, as I lay in the dark ward, I felt myself sinking further into a lonely well of sorrow. A distraught emptiness surrounded me. My fear was intense and at the same time reserved. It was a primitive, private fear: a fear that separated me from other human beings. None of the mothers knew anything about this fear. I could have told them, but they wouldn't have understood it. To them my baby looked like their babies, and I should have been very happy.

What I feared was nameless. I was haunted by a shadow, a cloud of incalculable dimension which I felt would some day burst, letting loose a terror that would swallow me up and drown me. But I didn't want to drown.

After the initial shock of realizing that there was something wrong, I felt no panic. I had wept all my tears in a few hours on that first night. Now I knew I was finished with deep weeping. There would be surface tears almost daily, but the depths of my being were preparing for a task that I knew I would be hard put to handle. I needed all my strength.

Slowly I put my mind in order and waited. Like a sailor preparing his craft for a storm, I battened down the hatches of emotion and self-pity and prepared to ride the hurricane by not resisting, by not fighting too hard against what would happen. I accepted what was in store for me and was determined to make the best of it. It is impossible to fight the whole ocean of circumstance. Sometimes it's easier to stay afloat by drifting in the heaviest currents. At best one can stay above water and this I was going to do. I did not want to sink.

After fourteen days in the hospital I took my unusual little boy home with a clean bill of health. I had fed him painstakingly and his weight was now four ounces above birth weight.

"Pretty good weight, really, for a baby who stands on his head to drink half the time," laughed the sister who helped me out to the car.

2

ELLEN, AS SHE HAD PROMISED, SHOWED A GOOD DEAL OF RESENT-ment towards the new baby. She didn't want him to use her pram or her baby bath or her old bassinet, and made no bones about it.

"Go back to the hostable," she told him, scowling, her hands on her hips.

When I breast-fed David Martin she sank down in a corner and sobbed.

But gradually she overcame her jealousy and began to take a lively interest in the baby. She started helping at bath-time by handing me the soap and the pins and eventually invited him to sleep in her cot with her—an offer he noisily declined.

David maintained his aloof, dignified manner. At eight weeks he showed no sign of recognizing my presence. On the other hand, he smiled disarmingly every time he saw a curved scroll which decorated the living-room wall. He reserved almost all of his interest and animation for this scroll—a black S-shaped pattern against the white wall. We were puzzled. It seemed eerie that a small baby could become so thoroughly delighted at the sight of a mere pattern on a wall and not recognize his own mother.

Not long after he arrived home from hospital, slight rashes began to appear on his face and the rest of his body seemed dry and flaky. His skin was extremely sensitive, even to the touch of my hair, which eventually I had to cut short, wash every day, and keep covered in an effort to ease his rash. He could not stand the slightest irritant. If I wore make-up or perfume his eyes watered and puffed up and he had difficulty in breathing. Everybody in the house gave up using talcum powder. As I couldn't ask my friends to refrain from using make-up I couldn't take him visiting. Sometimes when I left him outside a shop in his pram a stranger would stop to admire him and I would hear him wheezing and struggling for breath. The only safe place near by was the botanical gardens, at the end of our street, and every day I used to take David and Ellen for an outing there. Ellen used to feed the ducks and play in the "cubby houses", as she called the shelters.

I found it impossible to ease David Martin into any sort of routine. He didn't seem to know the difference between night and day, and he rarely slept. The first doctor I consulted about this advised me to administer more discipline.

By the time David was six months old he had developed other unusual ways. He could stay awake for fourteen hours at a stretch, sometimes hardly moving, apparently quite content to do nothing; then break out into frenzied crying for six hours at a stretch; then, for no apparent reason, laugh and frolic and giggle for hours on end.

Sometimes he seemed unaware of my presence; at other times he seemed to want me out of the way and if I tried to handle him he fought me. Sometimes he stiffened if I went near him, and resisted all my efforts to feed and bathe him. Sometimes he lay with his arms folded across his chest, and I couldn't change his clothes. When he was in these unresponsive moods I just had to leave him until the stiffness had passed. Sometimes I would have to wait ten minutes, sometimes an hour or more. It was absolutely impossible to establish a routine. If he was limp I could feed, bathe and dress him; if he was rigid I could not. When he was in an eating mood I usually fed him as full as he would go, because I never knew when he would eat again.

I worried constantly. I never knew from one day to the next what was going to happen. Although his strange behaviour was in itself cause for anxiety, my main problem was always keeping him alive—how to get him to take meals regularly.

By the time he was eight months old he had established his own routine and I was at a loss to know how to change it. Sleep from about 6 a.m. to 10 a.m., then wake for bath and food. Sometimes he would not allow me to feed and bathe him straight away; at other times he co-operated very well. He filled in his day pleasantly, gurgling and laughing and playing with a certain rattle. He could say "Mum, mum" and "Dad, dad" and "Bub, bub". Sometimes he showed an interest in me, but mostly he ignored me and, when I picked him up, kept his eyes glued to his rattle. Most of the day he seemed wrapped up in himself, playing with one toy or studying one moving object within his vision. After his park outing in the afternoon, he usually became noisy, shouting from time to time, then gradually working himself up into a state of extreme agitation. By about nine o'clock at night he was often restless and crying on and off. From then till the early hours of the morning he cried almost non-stop. The later the hour, the more hysterical he became. Nothing comforted him. He often cried all night without seeming to take a deep breath. Some nights I walked the floor with him; other nights I just let him cry. Whatever I did, it made no difference. He cried if I nursed him. He cried if I put him in his cot. He cried if I took him for a walk outside in his pram. If he was in a crying mood he cried, and that was all there was to it.

When he was ready to stop crying he simply stopped and became quite calm. There was no period of slowing down; he changed mood as though he had been switched off. By six o'clock in the morning he was always fast asleep, breathing evenly and looking like a happy, tired, resting baby. He could renew his strength very quickly, and four hours' sleep did him a lot of good. I often wondered whether he slept through the day as well with his eyes open. Some of the time he would lie very quietly, not moving, evidently restoring his strength in his own strange way. Perhaps one part of his brain slept while another part remained partially active.

Whenever he was in a co-operative mood he looked extremely intelligent, and wise beyond his years. At such times he might raise his eyebrows and seem about to join in some discussion.

He could sit up quite well at eight months, but without evident ambition. If I sat him up he sat up; if I laid him down he stayed down and made no attempt to get up. He had no curiosity about unfamiliar objects, remaining interested in his pattern on the wall. Music and water excited him very much. If I carried him into a room where the radio was playing I felt a shiver of excitement run through his body, and whenever I bathed him he splashed and shouted and jigged about till I lifted him out. After his bath there was water all over the room. If I left him in the bath long enough he would empty all the water onto the floor by furious splashing.

auditory

Every evening after work David, my husband, spent hours nursing and romping with him. Little David responded with reservations. After a good deal of effort on his father's part, he would work up a few chuckles. He was the kind of baby that took a lot of romping before he responded, but he did respond to his father. He responded more noticeably to touch than to voice.

sensory

At this time his feeding was a mechanical affair. If I placed a crust of toast in his hand he put it in his mouth, but if he dropped it he showed no emotion and made no attempt to look for it. If I placed the crust in his hands again he sucked at it, but didn't seem to care much one way or the other. He didn't appear to find pleasure in eating. If I placed a spoonful of food in his mouth he swallowed it, but without enthusiasm.

He put on weight rapidly and at this age looked beautiful. His skin, when I kept him away from powdered and perfumed visitors, was soft and fine and his cheeks were pink. The clinic sister thought him a particularly healthy-looking child, if somewhat unusual in manner. She detected in him a slight lack of interest in people, but didn't place any importance on this and didn't agree with me when I told her that there was something wrong with him.

When I took him to the clinic on injection days he always showed fear long before it was his turn. He sensed the atmosphere of tension; the crying of the other children made him stiffen, and from time to time I felt small tremors run through his body.

15

I just couldn't understand this baby. His behaviour after dark had me perplexed; I had never known anything like it. I took him to doctors, gave him sedatives, but nothing made any difference. More than one doctor thought I ought to administer more discipline and couldn't understand when I told them I couldn't get through to the child. I never found out why he screamed. He didn't seem in pain, and when in these disturbed moods he violently refused any form of refreshment.

At this stage of his life I spent a great deal of time nursing him—certainly more time than I had nursed my other two children when they were babies—but I don't think the attention registered with him. Several doctors who examined him at this time suggested that his problem could have been due to my not having nursed him enough, and they advised me to nurse him more.

I once asked a doctor about David's lack of interest in me and why he hardly ever smiled at me. The doctor bent over David. David looked him straight in the eye and gave him a most disarming smile. The doctor told me I had nothing to worry about, I had a charming baby.

There was always some embarrassment in going to doctors with David. They frequently gave me advice which anybody ought to have been able to carry out, but which I knew was impossible for me, though I couldn't explain why. I didn't know how to get David's co-operation. I knew what to do; what I wanted to know was how to do it. Whenever I complained that David wouldn't co-operate he would look up at the doctor as though he were the easiest child in the world to handle, and the doctor couldn't see why I was making all the fuss. It was pointless to tell doctors that I thought David was backward. When he was eight months old he could hum nursery rhymes, and at twelve months he had mastered several passages from complicated classical tunes as well as television themes. Though he *was* backward in some ways, it was not always apparent.

Just before David was nine months old I decided to take him and Ellen for a holiday at my parents' home in Toowoomba in Queensland. I wanted my mother to see David. I was tired and continually worried about him, and I thought she might be able to understand him. Also, I thought a rest from this night-owl baby would do my husband good, though he hated parting with us. My son Roley was already in Queensland for the school holidays, so we decided it was a good time for me to leave.

I was a bit apprehensive about the trip, but since David was still small enough to fit into a travelling bassinet I decided that it would not be too bad. I was expecting all sorts of things to happen with David aboard a plane. I didn't know whether he would scream all the way or not. I braced myself for the worst.

As it happened, he was no trouble at all. He endeared himself to the other passengers by snatching food from them. He showed an avid interest in everything they had on their food trays. Every time the hostess passed with food he grabbed himself a morsel. He showed no sign of shyness, and behaved as though he were in familiar surroundings. He had never behaved like this at home and had never reached for food before. And after the flight he didn't do it again.

When we arrived in Toowoomba everybody fell in love with the children. My father called the baby "Davey Boy", and bought a little car seat, and took David with him every time he went out on business. David liked it, and often tried to steer the car himself or change gears. He seemed quite aware that the levers and dashboard had something to do with making the car move. He seemed interested in everything. He took to watching television with a serious expression on his face, and he often thumped the piano with delight. Ellen, on the other hand, was a little shy and preferred to stay close to me.

My eldest brother was particularly impressed with little David. The first night we arrived, he took him over the road to see his wife's relatives. They were all surprised to see such an alert little baby. He showed no sign of tiredness and was not in the least shy. He didn't seem to mind who nursed him, and was placid in anybody's arms. They all agreed that they had never seen another baby quite like him. He was not a bit like the aloof baby I had described in my letters to Mother. The different environment seemed to have brought about a drastic change in his behaviour. He was highly intelligent for his age. He played games with Grandad's hat and kept putting it on his head to make everyone laugh. They called him "Personality Boy".

Within a week of our arrival in Toowoomba, however, he was covered from head to foot with a scaly rash, and was hardly recognizable. A local doctor diagnosed eczema.

In Toowoomba I got my first real opportunity to spend time concentrating on getting David to eat a variety of solids. But the new diet, plus the hard Toowoomba water used for bathing, along with the upheaval and excitement, seemed to be too much for him. He began to lie quietly most of the time, preoccupied with the ceiling or a window, gazing out with a tired look on his face. He didn't cry much, just whimpered from time to time, obviously in great discomfort.

Two weeks later, with his rash no better, both he and Ellen developed a fever which the doctor diagnosed as glandular fever. They were both extremely ill for many weeks. David slept a lot of the time and showed no interest in anything or anybody. He didn't seem to care whether I was there or not. I complained to my mother that he often didn't want me. "He may not want you," she replied, "but he certainly needs you." She was right.

Eight weeks later I brought the children back home to Melbourne. Ellen was still very shaky and had lost a lot of weight. David, though he had not lost weight, was still covered in eczema. Many times over the next few years I was advised to tie his hands to his cot or put his arms in splints to prevent him from scratching. I couldn't bring myself to do this; I felt that it would only distress him further. At times I put cotton mittens on his hands, but he always got them off and scratched till he was raw and bleeding. It was terrible, but I felt that it was the lesser of two evils.

It took about three months from our return home for the worst of the eczema to ease. At times it almost left him, but never quite. I went through months of experimenting with ointments and lotions and mixtures, and certain foods that were recommended by doctors and by the clinic. David's system, it seemed, could not break down the protein in his diet. His milk has always had to be boiled, even to this day. Until he was four years of age his stomach was as delicate as a

18

tiny baby's, and the milk had to be boiled for twenty minutes. Most of the time our house was like a hospital, dust-free and as hygienic as possible. No carpets or thick curtains, woollen garments barred.

By the time David was twelve months old his rash was under reasonable control. I had to keep him away from anything that would aggravate the condition, and give him a special diet. I also had to keep him smothered in ointments. I had to be constantly on the alert, but life was bearable if I kept my wits about me. This was difficult, because he was beginning to move about under his own steam and sometimes he touched surfaces that made his fingers bleed. We still had sleepless nights, but he cried less, humming tunes instead. He crawled gingerly at twelve months and walked cautiously at eighteen months. Though he had good co-ordination, he took no risks. The soles of his feet were very tender, and for many years he could only wear slippers. He never climbed up on anything if he had doubts about getting down safely. He mastered the stairs, and never once fell down them. He has never fallen over the way other toddlers do.

Ellen, the normal child, was adventurous, always climbing into places she couldn't get out of. She left no height unscaled, no cupboard unexplored. She always had skinned knees and often bruised herself. She was, however, an extremely loving child, and easy to handle. She helped with David from a very early age. She watched him crawling and learning to walk, and called me if she thought he was in danger. She worshipped him.

There were times when David's rash was so bad that he couldn't wear clothes at all and I had to keep him lying on a clean sheet in a heated room. The slightest irritation caused his skin to peel off, and his fingers bled if he touched anything. We spent a fortune on ointments and medicines. Strangely enough, throughout this eczema period, he continued to put on weight. He was a fine-looking child, and to outsiders, when he was not covered with rashes, he appeared perfectly normal and healthy.

The older he became, the longer his various moods seemed to last. He would go through stages of being quiet and solemn for days on end, then he would go through extremely gay days. Some days he would smile and chuckle constantly, though not often at people. Nobody seemed to notice this, and people would often think that they were the reason for David's merriment. Sometimes he could be stimulated by another person, but he would continue to laugh long after that person had left him. And he often laughed to himself whether there were people present or not. He still does this.

Looking after him took hours every day. My other two children got along as best they could. Ellen was marvellous, so loving and happy, accepting little David just as he was, with no complaints. There were many things she wanted to do and see, but we could rarely take David among crowds because of his allergies, and she understood this. She wanted to see ballet and opera and was most interested in music. When she was about three I took her to the ballet while her father took care of little David. She loved every minute of it. She even danced out in the aisle in time with the performers. Later she wanted to take up ice skating, but I couldn't take her to lessons; it was so difficult to find a baby-sitter for little David, and besides, I was worried about leaving him. I was always expecting his allergies to flare up or his rash to become worse. Nobody could feed him but me. I once left him and Ellen at a council crèche for a few hours while I kept a dental appointment and shopped. When I returned I found that Ellen had enjoyed the nursery and playground, but little David was covered in a weeping red rash from head to toe. He had screamed the whole time I was away, and nurses had been unable to feed him or even pick him up. They advised me to take him to a doctor because they thought there was something very wrong with him, and it was suggested that I should not bring him back again.

David's milk still had to be boiled for twenty minutes and his food had to be finely mashed and strained. He could not swallow easily and a lump in his food caused him to gulp and tears to come into his eyes as he swallowed. Often after swallowing a small lump he vomited. Whenever I tried him on unboiled milk it gave him stomach-ache, and I just had to continue with the baby diet. At the age of six he still couldn't digest unboiled milk. Yet when he ate he ate. He ate huge quantities of food, but it had to be fine. Boiled milk has always agreed with him. It was only after he took solids that the eczema problem arose. His system was very sluggish and he was often constipated.

At the age of eighteen months he developed tonsillitis and ear-ache. I took him to a pediatrician, who was marvellous with him. He was dreadfully upset by the injection she gave him, but the infection cleared up quickly. She prescribed extra vitamins for him—Vitamin C and a Vitamin B group, with a small quantity of folic acid. This seemed to improve his disposition. He was less jumpy when he was in responsive moods, and he became more confident.

One unfortunate result of the tonsillitis was that he became afraid of swallowing solids. He refused to eat, and for years afterwards drew back in fright every time he saw a spoon. He refused everything except his bottles. I was prepared to let him go at his own pace, little dreaming that it would be years before he would accept anything but liquid again. I persevered year after year, trying him with the spoon each day, and each day he turned away. I fed him everything through his bottles. I mixed strained meat and vegetables in a vitamiser with his boiled milk, adding vitamins, fluoride, and anything else he required. I knew this wasn't right, but I didn't know what else to do.

By the time David was two years old he appeared to be unaware of food, and even stopped holding crusts in his hands. His interests narrowed down to his bottles, two plastic soap-dishes, water, which continued to excite him, and the wheels of his stroller, which he spun round and round till his fingers bled.

There was never a period in his life when things went smoothly, but now began the most frightening period of all. He became less and less interested in the world around him till for some of the time he seemed to be in a sleepwalking state.

My son Roley had never been at ease with little David, and now the strangeness embarrassed him and he was unable to explain it to his friends. He had loved Ellen all through her babyhood and had never tired of romping and playing with her, but little David upset him.

As sure as Roley set up his homework books on the dining-room table little David would shout or cry or do something to distract him. Every time I sat down to talk over Roley's school difficulties with him I would be interrupted by little David's needing some sort of attention. If Roley prepared himself a sandwich after school, little David usually managed to spit on it while Roley was off guard. There was also the lack of sleep. Ellen usually managed to sleep through anything, but Roley had many disturbed nights.

The apartment house in South Yarra was deteriorating both as a dwelling and a business. When the lease was nearly up we started looking for fresh accommodation. This was even more difficult to find than it had been five years before, because we now had three children instead of one and we still had no money behind us. The South Yarra house, though conveniently situated for my husband's work and study, had been a financial disaster. Rooms seemed to be harder to let after little David was born. Tenants like to have their sleep, too, and people usually didn't stay long. In any case, after little David and Ellen joined the family we had found it necessary to take extra rooms for our own use. Repairs kept us constantly out of pocket. The floors of the downstairs rooms were rotting under the new lino aesthetically laid by the landlord before we moved in. Moisture had seeped through the lino over the years, and it was disconcerting to be standing talking to a tenant at my kitchen door, only to sink suddenly down to my knees through the floor. The lino covering made it hard for me to know which section of the floor was likely to go next.

To add to the confusion that reigned from time to time, our phone number had apparently belonged previously to the Portuguese Consulate. At all hours of the day and night I found myself trying to convince people from Portugal who spoke little English that I was not their Consul. These arguments, which continued during the entire five years of our tenancy, left me limp because I always lost. I made many attempts to find out the new number of the Portuguese Consul, but whenever I phoned Information I was told that my number was the number of the Portuguese Consul. Many times I thought of learning Portuguese—just enough words to extricate myself with—but I never did get round to it.

During those five years at South Yarra I discovered that my husband David, though a genius at criminology and a whiz at electrical work (he set up an involved system of extension wires and extra plugs all over the walls), was not much of a hammer-and-nails man. Shelves he built would fall down in the night and his cupboards would buckle in the early hours of the morning. One of his doors came off its hinges in my hand. But in any case, it always seemed to me a waste of time to interrupt his studies, which I considered most important, to repair a house that was falling down anyway.

Just before we moved David completed ten years of university study by gaining his Diploma in Criminology. He was the first person in Australia to take out this diploma, and he would now be able to provide conditions in which other students could conduct research and learn about prisoners. I was terribly proud of my husband.

During our stay in the South Yarra house there had been some sorrow, some happiness, and much laughter. All in all they were five good years. David and I were very much in love, and any year is a good year when you love somebody.

3

WE FOUND A HOUSE TO SUIT US IN BRIGHTON, AND MOVED JUST
after Christmas in 1963. It was a comfortable-looking brick
bungalow, well built, with a large garden; but after we
moved in we discovered that it needed a lot of repairs.

The landlord, to use his own words, was a "poor Greek
migrant, battling to survive in a new land", so David had to
set to work again with hammer and nails. Not long after we
moved in, the laundry floor fell through and the clothes-lines
fell down. The roof leaked during the first shower of rain.
The landlord had his own philosophy about leaking roofs:
when it's fine there's no need to mend them, and when it's
raining it's too wet. So David had to learn a smattering of
plumbing as well as carpentry.

I was so tied down with little David and had so little time
to think about anything other than my immediate surroundings that my immediate surroundings became more important
to me than they normally would have done. I have never
been very house-proud and will usually accept the ordinary
amenities without thinking much about them. At this time of
my life, however, such things as clothes-lines, stoves, and
refrigerators became all-important to me.

The children were pleased to have a large yard to play in.
Little David used to walk round and round the fence, looking up at the sky from time to time, humming tunes and

calling out. But most of his days now were spent splashing water, spinning wheels, and collecting matchboxes and drinking-straws. He had a little cache behind one of the gates in the back yard, and often sat there alone examining his treasures.

At Brighton my husband had to develop yet another talent: he made several pieces of furniture. I was fairly proud of the solid look he achieved with just a few pieces of timber, but Roley, somewhat more critical, said it reminded him of Stonehenge furniture. Over the next few years, however, we came to be thankful that my husband had used strong, heavy timber, because little David, as he grew older, spent a lot of time springing from one piece of furniture to another.

He was always changing, and at this age he progressed a little in some directions and regressed in others. A lot of the time he seemed almost a zombie. He still looked normal and his expression was often quite intelligent, but he seemed to be using only one part of his brain at a time. Sometimes I noticed that he didn't seem to feel pain as much as before, and he was not so receptive to music. He was still difficult to handle, but the difficulties were not always the same. Loud noises didn't register with him as they had previously done, and he was often oblivious of the presence of people. When he was two and a half he started pointedly turning his back on people. I felt that I had even less contact with him than before.

Sometimes he retired to his cot alone, lay on his back, held a little plastic pig above his face, and tried to pick out its bright blue eyes with his forefinger. He remained interested in this toy pig for about three years. He always drew away from fluffy toys and live animals.

He used to spit on this little pig. Indeed, he spat at any bright object that caught his eye, and became an expert shot. I used to dread visitors wearing jewellery. Little David would stare fixedly for a few moments, then draw a bead and spit at anything that sparkled.

In the Brighton house he had a room to himself for the first time, and, although Ellen was disappointed to lose him as a room-mate, he was much more content on his own. While he was sharing a room with Ellen I had been forced to place a blanket along the side of his cot so that he couldn't see her. This made Ellen most indignant, but it was the only way we could get any peace.

Ellen was three and a half years old by this time, and missed her South Yarra kindergarten. She now wanted to attend one at Brighton. Unfortunately, the nearest was a good two miles from our new home and there was no transport. Our old car was on its last wheels, and anyhow I couldn't drive. I was afraid to learn to drive by this time, there being so many things wrong with the car. Once when David was passing through Kew Junction the brakes failed, and each time we had the car repaired the garage man shook his head and told us it would be the last.

I wanted Ellen to attend kindergarten, not only because she was so keen, but because I felt that little David was a most unsatisfactory playmate for her. She tried hard to get on with him and constantly made overtures to him, but he rejected her. He often turned his back and grizzled when he saw her. I'm sure she did him a lot of good in the long run, but I didn't think it was fair for her to have such a one-sided relationship all the time. I wanted her to play proper games with children of her own age. She had not had much opportunity to play normally.

We found out where the kindergarten was, and I began to walk her to it every day. Little David made these trips a nightmare. He would sit quietly in the pusher for half the journey, then break into frenzied screaming and struggle to get out. I had to fight to hold him in, for whenever he got out of the pusher he would run as fast as he could, over roads, into oncoming traffic, anywhere. He would just scream and run. When I tried strapping him into the pusher he panicked and screamed. The more he screamed, the more his body became irritated, and he invariably finished up with a weeping red rash over the whole of his body.

I was on the point of giving up when a girl who lived near by, seeing my plight, offered to take Ellen in her car. Her own little boy, three-year-old Timmy, became good friends with Ellen, who was overjoyed to have such a responsive, imaginative playmate. He spent afternoons with her on the days they didn't attend kindergarten. His mother, her hands already full with her own small children, used to pick Ellen up every kindy day. Ellen would race out to wait for the car with half an hour to spare, her play-lunch packed in her little red shopping-basket. She got a lot of fun out of driving to kindy with a carload of other children.

When Timmy came to play with Ellen he told her he was the doctor come to cure the "children", as they called her dolls. This went over big with Ellen, and his visits always coincided with outbreaks of measles and broken limbs among her dolls. Timmy's father was also a doctor, so he always had an interesting supply of spent tubes and discarded phials with which to effect his cures.

While Dr Timmy worked diligently on the dolls' "mizzles" Ellen ran messages for him. She would rush into the kitchen where I was working, calling out, "Water!" After delivering the water to Timmy she would run back to the kitchen and call out, "Ointment!" A few minutes later she would be back, shouting, "Medicine!" The next call was usually for "lollies" or "biscuits".

After a good morning's work in the nursery, Dr Timmy would emerge soggy but important-looking with his stethoscope, and ask for his lunch of Vegemite swamiches and a drink of cordle.

Sometimes the two children wanted to include David in their game, but he wouldn't co-operate. He would often sit in the same room with them, but always apart, and often with his back to them. If they approached him he would get up, walk a short distance away, and sit down again.

Ellen invented a special country for little David to live in. It was called Double Holland, and David was its handsome prince. Whenever he did anything she couldn't understand she would say, "That's the way they do things in Double Holland. He's the handsome prince of Double Holland and he can do anything he likes." His name was Prince Audie of Double Holland and all his subjects loved him. His first court adviser was a Humpty-Dumpty-shaped fellow called Hon Sting, who was full of fun. He didn't have a head separate from his body but was shaped a bit like a gonk. His wife, who was also great fun, was "a lady called Sting". She was tall and thin. She and Hon were always trying to learn to waltz, but Hon was a terrible dancer, always out of step. Ellen used to double up with laughter when she told me about their latest dancing lesson. She taught the people of Double Holland many skills. They would come and ask her, "Ellen, how do you dance the waltz?" or, "Ellen dear, please tell us how to play the piano", or, "Ellen, please teach us how to build a road." She would agree to help them, but first she had to get permission from Prince Audie. The handsome prince always made a sign that she could go ahead, and she would then sit down in the garden and explain what the people wanted to know. Ellen was determined not to be bored. If there was nobody to talk to she made up playmates, but she always included little David and gave him a part that didn't require any effort.

One of Ellen's favourite games was "brides". She would dress up in yards of old mosquito net and carry a plastic flower bouquet. Then, clasping her favourite doll under her arm, she would wander round the yard calling out, "Who wants to marry me?" She held wedding ceremonies wherever little David happened to be standing. A most reluctant bridegroom, he would walk off when the ceremony was half over, but she kept after him. If he refused to stop playing with the wheels of the stroller she'd say, "That's the way princes in Double Holland get married, they twirl wheels during the ceremony."

The people of Double Holland were all unusually shaped and spoke a strange language. They were a bit like clowns, and could jump in the air and stay there as long as they liked. They could leap over fences and walk on water, and they could perform the most fascinating magic tricks—tricks that you could hardly believe. Double Holland was a paradise where children could do anything they wanted, and no matter how they behaved they were loved and admired and accepted. There was a little pink bow who lived in Double Holland and her name was Mimmy Barba and she was everybody's friend. She used to run all the messages. If you wanted an ice-cream you just had to call out, "Mimmy Barba, please bring me an ice-cream", and she would run off and get it for you.

Ellen was beginning to realize that little David was a bit different, because other children who came to play began to ask questions about him. Double Holland made it easier for her to explain his behaviour, and sometimes she told them he had a wild brain. The youngsters were interested in his wild brain, and asked many more questions. One day I heard a little girl ask Ellen, "Where did David get his wild brain?" She told her, "David got his wild brain from Double Holland and there aren't any more left, so if you want one you can't have one, because only the handsome prince is allowed to have one." The little girl was most impressed.

When David was two and a half I could see that he was developing unevenly. He was able to do many things that other children did at his age, but other things, simple things, he wouldn't even attempt. At times he regressed. He could climb in and out of his cot without the slightest difficulty and could balance on the edge without fear of falling. He could remember where he had put his soap-dishes weeks before. He could set his bike upside-down against the steps at exactly the right angle so that he could spin the wheel, but he as grew older made no attempt to ride the bike. If I placed him in the seat and set his feet on the pedals he shook with fear and seemed to have no idea what he was supposed to do. He had a very advanced sense of height and space and knew how to hoist himself up neatly onto a table without a chair if he wanted to reach an object; but somehow he seemed unaware that the furniture was there. He didn't have to look at an object before climbing on it. He seemed to go by feeling his way and yet he was very quick. He was nimble at slipping out of his clothes and discarding his shoes. He had no idea of how to play with toys, but would show interest in certain parts of a toy; for instance, he would spin the wheels of toy cars but make no attempt to push them along the ground.

Nobody except my husband knew what I was talking about when I tried to explain what I thought was wrong with the child. Though occasionally he still cried at night, more often he hummed tunes. He developed a mania for Beethoven's Fifth Symphony and would hum passages from it by the hour. Sometimes he would stop suddenly in the middle of a phrase and I would lie awake waiting for him to complete it. Often he would keep me waiting so long that I began to wonder whether he had suffocated or fallen into a coma. Then, just as I was beginning to think there must have been something really wrong with him, he would finish the phrase, taking it up exactly where he had left off. He never lost his place, never went out of tune, and each time he stopped it was in a different place, so that I was never prepared for it. It was a special form of torture.

Sometimes I thought he was retarded, at other times that he was clever. He could be clever and stupid at the same time, alert and dull in the same hour, weary and energetic in the same minute. He could jump at the slightest sound, yet not seem to hear thunder. He was a child of contradictions. Sometimes when I tried to romp with him he ignored me; at other times he chuckled if he heard me coming. If he had a sore throat he often laughed a lot. He rarely did anything that made sense to me.

Over the months I began to think of a word that described David's state. I didn't like the word and I realized that it represented what I had feared from the beginning. I had never heard it used to describe a baby, but I couldn't think of any other to take its place. Everything about David that worried me—his lack of communication, his strange expressions, the face that could be alert and blank almost at the same time, his fear of things that weren't dangerous and his lack of fear of things that could harm him, his lack of contact with reality, his strange way of looking at things, almost a distorted view—all these things pointed to one word in my mind: insanity. David was out of tune with me and with his surroundings. By the time he was two and a half I thought he was insane. This was what had frightened me the first time I handled him.

I was never entirely free of a nagging fear that his behaviour could have been caused by some chemical or glandular malfunction that could have been righted had I been able to explain the symptoms well enough to a doctor. I felt that there was some physical basis for David's deviant behaviour, something wrong with his system that was causing his brain to deteriorate, some sort of chemical reaction that was destroying his brain cells. I couldn't shake off the belief that some day his symptoms would be sufficiently pronounced to be understood by a doctor. But by then it might be too late. By then his brain might be damaged beyond repair. Day by day I watched him slipping away from me, retreating mentally. At times he still shrank from contact with other people; often he seemed unaware of what went on around him.

Strangely enough, his face seldom lost its mobile expression and sometimes he smiled to himself when he was alone. Often he appeared quite deaf, sometimes blind.

I had to face the fact that he was slipping away from me. I felt that I was losing him. I think I could have borne this if he had been going somewhere, but he wasn't. He was sinking into oblivion.

For a time I couldn't face people. I wanted to be alone. I realize now that I wanted to join David in his lonely world. But I couldn't do that; he didn't want me. And I was so tired. There were so many nights of broken sleep. My friends must have thought I was very strange about this time. I found it hard to talk to them; there seemed to be nothing to say, no colour to conversation, no light and shade in human relationships.

My feeling was not so much one of loneliness as of aloneness. There were plenty of friends, but I couldn't share my strange sorrow with any of them, and sometimes I was so busy caring for my husband and children that I almost forgot about it. Then it would return—the fear, the cold chill that struck deep. The fear to which I had now given a name would sweep over me and I would be desolate.

The winter we spent at the Brighton house was the coldest I have ever known. We were about a mile from the coast and our kitchen and laundry doors faced the beach with no protection from the icy winds and driving rain that swept across the back yard and under the doors. Little David's skin and diet problems meant that I had to spend a lot of time in the laundry and kitchen, shivering non-stop. Sometimes, when his rash was particularly severe, he couldn't wear clothes at all and heating became a big consideration. The old fireplaces in the house were extremely small and the chimneys wouldn't draw properly. I was afraid to leave the children in a room heated by the kerosene heater while I was in the laundry, and I couldn't take little David outside in the cold. The old house, though it looked pleasant, was not right for us, and we decided to look for another.

During the spring of that year, when little David was two and a half, my husband came home one day with some surprising news. While searching for a textbook in the university library he had come across a book about a rare childhood condition known as autism. The symptoms of this condition were similar to those exhibited by young David.

From then on, the thing that was wrong with David had a name. I was tremendously excited to find out that something was known about it, and we began collecting literature. The more we collected, the more confusing it became. There were dozens of symptoms all tied up with the same state, and many theories on the reasons for it.

After a while I realized that having a name for David's problem was not the big relief I had expected it to be. No doctor I spoke to had heard of it, and even when I explained it to doctors who handled David for childhood illnesses they couldn't grasp the extent of his disabilities. In any case, treatments for childhood ailments were completely without purpose when David's condition made it all but impossible for me to carry them out.

This baffling, frustrating condition remained the mystery it had always been, only now it had a name. Some of the reasons given for autism worried me dreadfully. It had been suggested that it was a result of mothers being cold to their children and not showing them love; that because some mothers, incapable of giving love, remained aloof from their babies, the babies could not develop into normal people. I now had a new anxiety—one that had never entered my head before. Was it my fault that my son was so dreadfully damaged?

My husband assured me that it wasn't, but, although I trusted his knowledge, the thought persisted somewhere at the back of my mind.

All through these worrying years my husband continued to play with little David every evening after work, and little David continued to respond in a stilted way. His movements were clumsy, and sometimes he bumped his head against his father without seeming to realize that he was so close. When he was alone his movements were natural and flowing and he had good control over his limbs, but whenever he tried to move with or towards a human being he became unsure of himself and hesitated.

Reading about autism, I discovered that the word had a Greek origin, meaning *self*. An autistic child was one who seemed to be preoccupied with self, withdrawn.

I learned that the condition had first been clearly described in 1943 by Dr Leo Kanner, at that time director of the Child Psychiatry Clinic at the Johns Hopkins Hospital, Baltimore. Dr Kanner's original paper, based on case histories of eleven children, was entitled "Autistic Disturbances of Affective Contact", and he later developed the term "early infant autism". He used this term because each of the eleven children appeared to be withdrawn, aloof. They lived in what seemed an isolated dream-world, unable to contact or communicate effectively with other people.

This syndrome is extremely difficult to diagnose or describe, because most, if not all, of the symptoms appear at some time or other during the development of normal children. Young children frequently withdraw from reality and play at make-believe; but slowly, over the years, they learn to differentiate between truth and fantasy.

In 1961 a working party in the United Kingdom under the chairmanship of Dr Mildred Creak set out nine criteria for diagnosing infant autism:

1. Gross and sustained impairment of emotional relationships with people.

2. Apparent unawareness of his own personal identity to a degree inappropriate to his age; for example, self-directed aggression.

3. Pathological preoccupation with particular objects or certain characteristics of them without regard to their accepted functions; for example, spinning everything that can be spun.

4. Sustained resistance to change in the environment and the striving to maintain or restore sameness.

5. Abnormal perceptual experience (in the absence of discernible organic abnormality); for example, insensitivity to pain.

6. Acute, excessive and seemingly illogical anxiety, as a frequent phenomenon.
7. Speech either lost or never acquired, or showing failure to develop beyond a level appropriate to an earlier age; for example, phrases may convey no sense—may be echo speech.
8. Distortion in motility patterns; for example, overactivity, rocking, spinning.
9. A background of serious retardation in which islets of normal, or near normal, or exceptional intellectual function or skill may appear.

Two of these characteristics are common to all autistic children—numbers one and seven.

I discovered that there was a diversity of opinions concerning autism. I have been told that it is a symptom, a way of behaving that may be associated with any one of a group of disorders.

I continued to ask questions and to read and puzzle over this condition. But nowhere could anyone show me how to administer four or five doses of medicine a day at four-hourly intervals to a child who wouldn't swallow. If David became ill and needed medicine I had a real problem on my hands.

Not long after we began reading about autism my husband was asked to give a talk on the subject to a kindergarten mothers' club. It was difficult to know how to make the condition understandable to people who had no previous knowledge that such a thing existed and no training to enable them to grasp its subtleties and complexities.

David began his talk by giving a simplified version of Dr Mildred Creak's nine points:

1. Gross and sustained impairment of emotional relationships with people.
2. Apparent unawareness of personal identity leading; for example, to self-directed aggression.
3. Extreme preoccupation with objects or characteristics of them; for example, spending long periods spinning wheels.
4. Resistance to change of routine or change of position of objects.
5. Disturbances of perception with no apparent physical

34

reason; for example, insensitivity to pain, or cold, or loud noises.

6. Frequent attacks of acute anxiety for no discernible reason.
7. Speech either lost or never acquired, or underdeveloped —may be echo speech.
8. Unusual patterns of movement; for example, over-activity, rocking, spinning.
9. Retardation of mental development with perhaps some areas of normal or exceptional ability.

He went on: "These nine points give a good picture of an autistic child, but they are by no means all present in all autistic children, and some of them are present in non-autistic children. Some of them can be interpreted in different ways, and most of them are often found in normal children to some extent; the diagnosis becomes a matter of degree.

"Take, for instance, 'resistance to change'. Small, normal children often insist on having the same nursery rhyme sung to them over and over, night after night at the same time, or the same bedtime story told repeatedly, without deviation. And sometimes when they play hide-and-seek they want to hide in the same place each time and they want you to hide in the same place as well when it is your turn to hide. However, the parents of an autistic child are seldom in doubt that they have a sick child, even though they may not know the name of the disease.

"At first the most noticeable characteristic is the impairment of emotional relationships, the feeling that the child is cut off by a 'glass wall', that his mind is beyond our reach. He keeps his distance, remains aloof, and avoids eye-to-eye contact with other people. He shows little awareness that other people exist. But often the child grows out of this stage, at least to a degree, and then we find that the barrier to communication is the autistic child's difficulties with language.

"There is no real consensus of opinion among the experts working in this field. Some think that autism is a variety of schizophrenia, some think that the symptoms can be attached to children with different problems, ranging from schizophrenia to mental retardation. Different researchers may, indeed, be working with different kinds of children.

"Dr Michael Rutter, of London University, distinguishes between autism and schizophrenia in a number of ways. Firstly, the sex ratio is different, with about four autistic boys to each girl, while with schizophrenia numbers are about equal. Secondly, a high proportion of parents of autistic children are of superior intelligence and socio-economic status, while parents of schizophrenic children come from all groups and classes. Also, schizophrenia is relatively common in the families of schizophrenics but is rare in the families of autistic children. Mental subnormality is more common among autistic children than among schizophrenics, but delusions and hallucinations are rare in autistic children while they are common in schizophrenics. There are differences, too, in patterns of test results and in the courses of the two diseases.

"It is also possible to distinguish between autism and mental subnormality. Although it is true that autistic children function at the level of subnormal children, in fact some of them have a very high intelligence and many are normal. It is not easy to assess their intelligence. Tests do not measure the intellectual apparatus we were born with. They measure the level at which we function now, and this depends (a) on our basic intellectual apparatus, and (b) on the way this is modified by learning and experience. Some psychologists think this modification takes the form of actual physical changes, but computer technology suggests that these are not necessary.

"It is clear that autistic children may have normal intellectual apparatus, but as they are cut off from normal experience and learning the normal modifications do not take place. Furthermore, if these modifications do not take place at the proper stage of the child's development the child cannot catch up afterwards and so probably cannot ever achieve the standards for which he had the potential at birth. It seems likely that there is a particular time when the body is ripe for each particular development, and if the development does not take place the organism cannot thereafter catch up in the normal, natural, and easy manner.

"The main theoretical division is between those who believe that autism is mainly inborn—the result of, for example, brain damage or defect, chromosomal abnormality, hormone deficiency, or simple inheritance—and those who believe it stems mainly from life experiences such as faulty handling or some sort of trauma. Of course, neither school of thought would say that it comes entirely from nature or entirely from nurture, but each lays more stress on one particular aspect.

"Presumably, some children are born with a disposition towards autism, which is realized under certain conditions. Perhaps all children could become autistic, but some succumb more easily than others. Frequently mothers are able to say from the first time they hold their babies that the babies are 'different', do not respond normally. However, to outside observers their pattern of development is not obviously abnormal until some stress situation appears to trigger off the full-blown syndrome.

"It has not yet been possible to demonstrate a physical basis for the disease, although the ratio of four autistic boys to every autistic girl strongly suggests something of this nature.

"Autistic children rarely if ever are born to obviously autistic parents. One reason for this is that autistic children seldom recover sufficiently to marry and have children. The percentage of autistic children having autistic brothers and sisters appears to be too low for the disease to be hereditary.

"No chromosomal abnormalities have been discovered in autistic children, nor is there any evidence which gives rise to the suspicion of chromosomal abnormality. By contrast, in the investigation of mongolism several clues pointed towards the chromosomes long before the abnormality was discovered.

"Brain damage seems more likely, at least in some autistic children. And by brain damage we don't necessarily mean the type of damage caused by a blow to the skull. The brain can be damaged during birth by a haemorrhage, an accumulation of blood pressing on the brain. It can also be harmed by blocking the oxygen supply, which causes a choking of the cells. To function normally the brain uses up oxygen, carbohydrates (sugar) and fat. Any imbalance in the supply of these elements could damage the brain. A small obstacle in the pathways of the lungs of a new born baby could cut off the oxygen supply for a few minutes and damage the brain permanently.

"Brain damage can sometimes be discovered by using a machine called an electroencephalograph. Electrodes are attached to the skull and electric waves given off by the brain are registered on a graph. This is called an E.E.G. test. Another test is carried out by injecting air into the spinal canal. The air then accumulates in spaces round the brain. Certain types of damage can then be detected by X-ray.

"Some brain injuries lead to behaviour indistinguishable from autism, and some autistic children later show clear evidence of brain damage. Furthermore, the combination of perceptual and cognitive difficulties with language suggests brain injury, although these difficulties can occur in children exposed to extreme social isolation. Many autistic children show absolutely no signs of brain damage, when given tests of the type already mentioned, and where damage is found it seems similar to damage in other children who do not become autistic.

"It has also been suggested that because of brain peculiarities autistic children either over-react or under-react to general stimulation from outside.

"Dr Rutter has suggested that 'the basic defect in infantile autism is an impairment in the comprehension of sounds'. In other words, the language disorder becomes the basis for the disease rather than merely a symptom of it. The difficulties in perception of sound may be accompanied by other perceptual defects.

"Another theory is that autism can be caused by faulty family relationships, the emphasis being on 'refrigerated' parents or 'cold and detached' parents. It has been demonstrated in many cases that this is not true. In other cases it is not clear whether the parents' attitude was the cause of the autism or the result of years of strain in trying to care for an autistic child.

"Dr Bruno Bettelheim considers that autism results from an extreme negative feeling shown by the parent. The child lacks speech or emotional expression because it does not picture its parents as receptive. The child's brothers and sisters are not affected because the parents reject only the one child. This hypothesis cannot be discarded; nor is there any real evidence to support it. Possibly it is relevant in some cases.

"Because of the wide variations of the autistic state from child to child, the treatment offered is specific to the particular case. Treatment also depends on the orientation of the therapist. If he follows in the line of Freud, Goldfarb, Bowlby, and Bettelheim, he will want to try to improve the mother's relationship with the child. This, of course, can be infuriating to the mother who, sometimes to the exclusion of her other children, has lavished a disproportionate amount of care and affection on the strange little person she has brought into the world.

"The family that has an autistic child cannot live as other families do. In many cases the parents never go out together in the evenings. One of them must stay with the small tyrant. Brothers and sisters learn to expect their treasures to be broken and scattered, to live with embarrassing comments from other children.

" 'Treatment' does not aim so much at cure as at adjustment. The autistic child and his family can rarely be brought to a normal state. Even if the causes of the autism were known and corrected, the child could not make up for the lost years. He rarely reaches the stage where he is not considered at least 'odd'.

"Tranquillizers are sometimes given to tone down the overactivity of the autistic child who wants to shout and jump and play all night, keeping the rest of the family awake. Otherwise, drugs do not appear to be useful.

"The main frustration to a cure for autism is the language difficulty. Those children who learn to speak and understand make reasonable progress. 'Operant conditioning', a technique developed mainly by Skinner in America, relies on rewarding the child each time he makes a correct verbal response. Some successes have been claimed for this technique, but its effects, if any, are often short-lived."*

This talk of David's aroused considerable interest and many people phoned us afterwards. Some expressed amazement that children could display schizophrenic symptoms.

* For a fuller discussion of operant conditioning, see Chapter 7.

Some told me they had always thought schizophrenia meant a split personality of the Jekyll-Hyde type: good one day, bad the next. The split is really that between the reason and the emotions. A schizophrenic person can show emotion, but often the emotion is divorced from reason. He may laugh at the sight of a tragic accident, while everyone else on the scene is crying. He can be afraid of some imagined threat, but show no fear of actual danger. The emotions he shows don't tie up with the world around him. Of course, this is a very simple explanation: there are many types of schizophrenia and many phases of the illness.

One account I read of schizophrenia described it as a bio-chemical abnormality where certain secretions of the adrenal gland fall out of balance. One experiment showed that certain substances found in the urine of schizophrenics, but not present in normal people, caused laboratory rats to behave in an unbalanced manner.

Some autistic children are found to have abnormally high concentrations of lead in the bloodstream, but it is not known whether this is due to defective metabolism or increased ingestion of lead. Little David's urine test showed no chemical abnormality.

On learning that a predisposition towards mental illness can be inherited, I checked my own family history and David's, but could find no trace of mental illness on either side.

After living in the Brighton house for a year, we started searching in earnest for a house to buy. We had finished paying for a block of land in an outer suburb, but because it would take us a long time to save enough money to start building on it and because we could not raise a bank loan we decided to sell the land and use the price we got as a deposit on a ready-built house.

Houses in outer suburbs were cheap, so that's where we began our search, taking off in our old car every week-end after the Saturday-morning shopping scramble.

Little David was much easier to handle if his father came, too. He loved the car, and we could leave him sitting on the back seat while we looked at houses. He didn't mind being

40

David, aged sixteen months, is difficult
to photograph. He keeps making a
dash for the duck-pond. Caught at
last, he will not look at his father, but
busies himself with the shiny metal
on his stroller.

At two and a half, David
will not join in Ellen's
game, but sits idly
flicking sand.

The photographer managed to catch us all together just before
little David made a dash for freedom and had to be chased
round the block.

left in the car at all, and relaxed in his seat with a look of satisfaction on his chubby face. Of course, if we took him out of the car he would make one of his mad dashes for destinations unknown.

One Monday morning, just after my husband left for work, an agent in the outer suburb in Ringwood phoned to say he had a house that would probably suit us. It was in fairly good condition, had been painted outside, and met all our other stipulations.

I wasn't keen on making the trip to Ringwood without my husband to help me, and since I knew he would be busy all day I asked the agent if we could come out the following Saturday. He told me that the owners of the house were in a hurry to sell and that there were other prospective buyers, so I decided to go out at once with Ellen and David.

The trip out went well enough; the children were happy on the train; and the house was the most suitable I had seen so far. I settled for it on condition that David agreed.

On the train going home I tried feeding little David his bottles (I had tried several times while we were at Ringwood, but he would not drink properly). He took a few sips, just enough to keep him going. He was becoming restless. I kept my fingers crossed, hoping he wouldn't start a hysterical outburst before we arrived home.

We were approaching Richmond, where we had to change trains, when he began to struggle to get out of the stroller, and I had to fight to keep him in it. As the train pulled in to Richmond he started screaming and clawing at everybody and everything. The train was packed with schoolchildren. While I was struggling to get to the door little David grasped a leaning-post and I had to battle to make him let go. Ellen was crying and calling out, "Hurry up, Mummy! The train's going to start." I finally got to the door, through the crowds of children, and fell out on the platform with David and the stroller just as the train moved away—with Ellen still on it. As it pulled away I caught a glimpse of her struggling to jump off. Somebody dragged her back. As the train rounded the bend I could see my handbag trailing outside the door.

I got to my feet and with tears streaming down my face raced up to the ticket-collector and told him what had happened. He was a New Australian lad and couldn't understand what I was yelling about. Shouting to be heard above David's screaming, I got him to phone Flinders Street station for me. I did the talking, and asked the man at the other end to put Ellen with the guard on the next train back for Richmond.

Little David continued to yell and beat his head with his fists and kick me every time I came within reach of him. I was terrified he would escape from the stroller and jump off the platform onto the line. Trains were coming and going every minute or so, and there were crowds of people rushing back and forth.

When the next train from Flinders Street pulled in I hurried to the guard's van. Ellen flew into my arms with my handbag slung over her shoulder. She cried and cried. "Why did you leave me on the train?" she kept shouting. I tried to explain to her that the ticket-collector had flagged the train on too soon and that it had been too late for him to stop it when he saw me falling out.

Eventually she calmed down, but as we pushed our way out of the station to look for a taxi she shouted at the ticket-collector, "You silly bloody flag-waver!"

4

WE MOVED TO RINGWOOD TWO WEEKS BEFORE CHRISTMAS. THERE
was a lot to be done. The fence and gate had to be made
secure, for although little David couldn't unlatch gates he
could push on them. Neighbours helped out and alerted me
if he escaped. He seemed not to notice or care that we were in
a different house, and went about his own affairs as usual. We
had brought his collection of drinking-straws and matchboxes,
of course, and he soon had them cached behind a pine-tree
near a side fence.

My husband strung up a swing between two old pine-trees.
Ellen was delighted. Little David couldn't quite understand
it at first, but as the months passed he began to watch Ellen
swinging, out of the corner of his eye, and I felt that he was
interested and was biding his time. Eventually he did give it
a try, but, on the whole, during that first year at Ringwood
he was at his least responsive. He moved about the house and
yard in what appeared a semi-sleepwalking state, completely
preoccupied with his own activities, oblivious again of other
people.

As our first winter approached we realized that the heating
in the house was inadequate and that if we were going to
keep little David from catching pneumonia we'd have to
install a more efficient system. He had suffered several bouts
of asthma while he had a cold, and I was apprehensive every

time he started to sniffle. He learned to remove his clothes that year, and began to spend most of his time naked. All through the winter I spent my days dressing him and he spent his days undressing.

We eventually installed a combined central heating and hot-water service; although the payments were crippling we felt it was necessary. Little David's medical and chemist bills had been staggering, but after the heating system was installed he rarely caught colds and became much easier to live with.

Throughout the winter he searched constantly for water, and the sound of a tap being turned on anywhere in the house brought him racing to the scene. He also developed a passion for the theme tune of the television feature "Z Cars". As soon as he heard the kettle-drums that lead in to it, he would run to the television set, and when the theme was over he would race round the room, crying and screaming. Sometimes when he became very agitated he would thump his head on the floor or furniture, and I often had to slip a pillow under his head to ease the blows.

His father studied him and often tried to play with him. He read a great deal about autism and kept in touch with people who worked among disturbed children. He was absorbed in little David's behaviour, and noticed many things that I didn't. His training in psychology gave him an inkling of the type of problems that lay ahead of us, but he didn't draw conclusions or make any comment without considering every phase of his son's behaviour.

Now, as little David approached his third birthday, his strangeness was obvious to everyone. He still looked normal, but he was noticeably not "with" the rest of the world. And as well as his aloofness he began to adopt unusual mannerisms. He hopped instead of walking, and when studying an object he often flicked it back and forth and looked at it out of the corner of his eye. He also made unusual noises with his mouth. By blowing through tightly compressed lips, he would make a sound like a trumpet. I find this impossible to do, but he is expert at it.

At times during that first year at Ringwood I became dreadfully depressed by signs of further withdrawal in him. If he was going to keep regressing as he grew older, the future

44

seemed grim. I couldn't bear to think of what lay ahead.

He still insisted on taking food through his baby bottles, only now he took sixteen bottles a day. (Later I had to increase the number to twenty.) He still couldn't digest unboiled milk and was sick if he swallowed a lump in his food. I often tried to feed him new foods with a spoon, but he seemed not to see me or the food or the spoon.

The endless round of preparing his food each day and washing huge piles of bedclothes was wearing me down. He slept naked, unable to wear plastic pants because of the persistent eczema. Even when his skin was clear the seams in his pyjamas made his skin bleed. I was tiring badly, and almost stopped hoping.

He was sleeping worse than ever. He could jump and shout right through the night. Switching out the lights made no difference. Even in the dark he could jump all over the furniture without falling. He seemed to have an inbuilt radar system. We were loath to drug him because we didn't want to slow down his reasoning or restrict what awareness he had, but we realized that we had to do it. We tried every kind of sedative. All they did was to make him drunk and miss his footing and fall over. I've never found anything that would put him to sleep.

I was also worried about my son Roley. He had joined the Air Force, but was still very unsettled. My first marriage, years earlier, had been a wartime one, and I had never been happy. Roley was born at the end of the Second World War and the first five years of his life had been most disturbed. My unhappy marriage had left its mark on him.

Having little David made it impossible for me to devote the necessary time to either of my other children. Ellen got by well enough, but Roley could never take little David's presence with ease. Many times when I should have talked with Roley I was either not available or just too tired. Some of Roley's friends, however, took to little David without worry. One of them said he had the greatest admiration for any kid who could get away with urinating where he pleased, paid no attention to authority, could blow like a trumpet, and hop as if on a pogo stick.

Not long after he joined the Air Force Roley bought a car

45

on hire-purchase. One Friday, while trying to drive overnight from Adelaide to Melbourne on week-end leave, he smashed the car up. He was in hospital for two weeks in South Australia and didn't let me know because he didn't want to worry me. He knew that no one else could feed little David. When I heard about this I felt awful. I knew Roley needed me.

As our second Christmas at Ringwood approached, I noticed little David sitting on the front veranda each day when the postman blew his whistle. I didn't know why he was doing this. Perhaps, I thought, he was interested in the whistle. He was certainly interested in something. One day he came running into the house just after the postman's whistle blew. In his hand was a letter. He took it into the nursery, lay on his bed, held it up above his head, and said, "Card."

I could hardly believe my ears. I sat beside him on the bed and tried to persuade him to say it again. I opened the envelope and handed him the brightly decorated card, saying, "Card", over and over again. It was useless. He just looked at me coldly as though he had never seen me before. I couldn't believe that he'd say a word once and then not bother with it again, but that's just how it was.

Several months later a friend called to take me shopping. As I was dragging little David out to the car he said, "Car car." He refused to say it again that day, but when my friend called the following week he said, "Car car", again. That was the last time he said the word, but from then on he always recognized it. This didn't make it any easier for me to get him into the car if he didn't want to come. When I said, "Car, car", he would come with me if he wanted to and run away if he didn't. Either way, though, I knew that he understood "the word". I had to learn never to say "the word" in his hearing if I were not going to take him in the car, because if I did, and he wanted to go, he would show his disappointment by beating his head on the cement path.

Not long after this he learned another word, though he wouldn't say it himself. The word was "bath". Whenever I said it he would come to the bathroom if he wanted to get into the bath or run like fury if he didn't. Having him understand a few words didn't make life easier, but it gave us fresh hope.

Just after his fourth birthday he spoke again.

Every night when I put the children to bed I would kiss Ellen and try to kiss David, who would never allow it. Then, as I went to the door, I would call out, "Nigh nigh"—which had been Ellen's good-night call when she was very small. When I put David to bed he would always place a pillow over his head and snuggle under the bedclothes, though he used not to stay there long. He paid no attention when I called out, "Nigh nigh." One night, hearing no noise in the nursery, I tiptoed in. Seeing Ellen asleep and David's pillow over his face, I began to tiptoe out again without speaking. Before I reached the door David raised the corner of the pillow, called out, "Nigh nigh", and quickly pulled the pillow down again. He has not said it since.

One evening I was calling him to go to bed and he kept running away from me. I finally blocked his path and called out, "Nigh nigh." He dodged by and cried, "No no", in the same tone of voice as I had used. Another time he said, "No no", when I was trying to wipe him dry after his bath. He has not spoken since.

The lack of speech is of course the severest of handicaps. Without meaningful speech the child has no interchange of ideas with others. He can't sort out his views or widen his horizons without the ability to discuss and assess other people's impressions. He stays in a mental rut.

When David's digestive system began to trouble him again, as it did from time to time, I took him to a pediatrician to whom David's old specialist, who had gone overseas, had referred us.

Although I often took David to general practitioners, it had been twelve months since we had seen a specialist, and he had changed a lot in that time. He had always been very well behaved previously when visiting the specialist and, although he had not spoken at the age of three, he could hum tunes and didn't appear retarded. When we arrived at the new doctor's surgery David behaved in the oddest manner and for the first time showed himself in his true colours in front of a doctor. He sprang from chair to chair, crouched in a corner, cried, refused to be examined, climbed over the doctor's desk and shuffled papers and files to the floor. He also threw him-

47

self at the large plate-glass window several times. The examination was extremely difficult; David was as slippery as an eel.

The doctor referred me to a child psychiatrist. He also suggested a further blood test, and this proved to be quite an ordeal. It took all my strength to hold him still while a sample of blood was extracted from his arm. I thought that something might show up in his blood, since a lot of research had been done since his first blood test when he was born.

The results showed no abnormality. I suppose I should have felt relieved, but this negative outcome left me feeling flat. Had some abnormality shown up in the blood cells it is most unlikely that it would have helped David, because there would probably not have been any cure for it, but it would have given me a reason for his behaviour.

So I began visiting the psychiatrist at the Children's Hospital as directed and David was placed in the hands of a competent therapist. He was so disturbed by this time that we decided against having any more tests for the time being. The therapist gave him play therapy to ease his anxiety and she studied him and tried to understand him. On our first visit David just lay on the floor and cried and kicked, but after a few visits he was won over and began to feel at ease. It was a relief for me to talk to a doctor who had a grasp of David's problems, but I still believed that there was something out of balance in his system and felt ill at ease at not knowing what it was. For the time being, however, I had to settle for allowing the therapist to try and help him modify his behaviour and, when he was ready, provide him with the opportunity to learn whatever he was capable of learning.

Just before Christmas of 1966 a telegram arrived saying that my father had died of a heart attack.

I couldn't believe it. He was seventy-two, but had always been extremely fit. I was numb with grief. I longed to go to Queensland to comfort my mother, but I knew I couldn't make the trip with little David in tow. I couldn't go out, I couldn't take my eyes off him. Just to keep him alive was almost a twenty-four-hour-a-day job. My two older brothers lived close to Mother, and my youngest brother flew up from Melbourne. I stayed behind, frustrated and angry because I couldn't go to my own father's funeral.

For several months before his death Father had been writing that he wanted me to visit him. He had undergone minor surgery and said he was feeling tired. I knew he wanted to talk to me, but I kept refusing to go to him because of little David. And while I was thinking about it, my father died.

My love for my father was part of my personality, something that would never leave me; yet when he died all I could do was send a wreath.

I felt bitterness for the first time. I knew I could have left David in an institution for a week, but I was afraid of what this might do to him. I was utterly miserable, torn between anxiety for my mother and concern for little David. My depression lasted for months, and, to make matters worse, twice during that time little David came into contact with something he was allergic to.

On the first occasion, he evidently touched some peanuts I had put out in a bowl for a visitor, and then rubbed his face with his hands. Anyway, I soon heard him wheezing, and found him lying on his bed in the nursery, his face swollen to twice its normal size, his eyes glazed. He could not get his breath. His nasal membranes must have been swollen, and he was blue round the lips. His distress was frightening. We phoned our doctor, who was waiting with injections ready when we arrived at the surgery. All the way to the surgery David fought me while he struggled to get his breath. The doctor must have known exactly what to give him. Within ten minutes of receiving the first injection he was sleeping, breathing deeply and normally. The next day he was dopy, but within three days the swelling had disappeared.

On the second occasion, he touched some eggshells and rubbed his face with his hands. Soon after, his eyes were protruding like golf balls and his forehead was huge. Again he couldn't breathe, and struggled all the way down to the doctor's. And again the doctor had the right injection ready.

At this time David was beginning to touch things again, after a few years of ignoring them. This was a good sign, but

49

it meant that I had to be doubly careful that he didn't touch anything that might affect him. Ellen loved bread and peanut butter, but we had to guard it like dynamite and keep it hidden from little David. She had to remember never to leave a crust of bread on a plate where he could reach it.

Once before, when he was about two years old, we were visiting friends on the other side of town, and he had collapsed to the floor not long after our arrival. He appeared to be doped, and didn't wake up for two days. The doctor decided that he must have breathed in something he was allergic to, possibly the odour of a plant.

Looking back at this period, I know I was continually worried and on edge, unable to help myself. I must have been pretty poor company, but my husband was unfailingly tolerant and patient and I loved him more as the years went by. I didn't quite realize how selfish I had become until I heard about the Tokyo trip.

The Government had offered to send David for three months to the United Nations School of Criminology in Tokyo, and he had turned the offer down without giving it a second thought. He knew I couldn't go with him, and he had no intention of leaving me. I decided he had given up enough opportunities because of little David and me. I insisted that he should go. He took a lot of persuading that I could cope for three months on my own, but I was determined. Finally he agreed to go.

As the day of his departure drew near I began to worry myself sick. How on earth was I going to manage? I dreaded having to part with my husband. I made several resolutions. I decided to get my driving licence in his absence (we now had a roadworthy car), and I was determined to try writing again. I had not written a story for years, and I knew that it would be good therapy for me, and ease my loneliness.

My first problem cropped up several days after David's departure, when the cheque for his Tokyo expenses arrived from the Department of External Affairs. Since he hadn't been able to draw against it before leaving, he had borrowed the amount from the bank and taken all the money he and I had had on hand to meet the monthly expenses. Knowing that the cheque would arrive soon after his departure, I had paid all the monthly bills on the strength of it. But the day after I deposited the cheque the bank rang me to say that it was no good: it was unsigned. This was quickly righted, of course, but in my overwrought state I panicked and broke down and wept. I knew I was being stupid, but I felt utterly helpless. I was isolated and unable to leave the house. I had to keep asking neighbours to help out all the time, and I hated doing this.

Soon after David left I phoned a driving school. Knowing that there would be difficulties about little David, I was apprehensive. I told the instructor that I would have to take my son along.

"No trouble," he said cheerfully.

"But he's autistic," I said.

"That'll be quite all right," he said, just as cheerfully.

Poor man! After the first lesson he was a mess. What with my driving and with little David spending the whole hour shouting and calling out and jumping up and down in the back seat and spitting at the back of his neck, he was driven to distraction.

"Well, I warned you David was autistic," I said.

"I thought you said *artistic*," he said.

I knew it would be useless to continue lessons with little David in the back seat, so I phoned the Ringwood Council to find out if they had some sort of baby-sitting service staffed by intrepid women. I learned that a group of women from the local Methodist Church did voluntary baby-sitting, the fees going to charity. I was given the number of Mrs Wigley, who turned out to be an angel. She was kind and gentle with little David, and most conscientious. Although she only vaguely understood his condition at first, she eased her way into his confidence until I could leave him with her for an hour. She could not undertake responsibility for him for longer. I know she found it a strain. But an hour was enough, and a tremendous relief.

I went at my driving lessons like a tornado. It took me twelve lessons of running over nature strips, scraping tyres along gutters, and grinding gears to convince the instructor that I was ready for a try at my licence. The examiner was evidently in a good mood that day, and I passed. The instructor was as relieved as I was. I was ruining his car.

When I got home after the test I was trembling all over, but floating on a cloud. Within about three weeks I had lost my nervousness and was driving all over Melbourne. Little David took on a new lease of life, too. He loved riding round in the back of the car, and I tried to take him for a little outing each day to relieve the monotony.

I used to leave him in a car-park while I shopped. One day a friend who happened to pull in to the car-park saw him naked, springing from the roof of one car to the next. She caught him, and after a great struggle returned him to my car and locked all the doors. I still don't know how he got out in the first place. Some child must have opened a door for him, because he couldn't do this himself at the time.

Anyway, I soon had to start thinking of something else to do with him while I went shopping. Apart from the fact that he might escape, he became bored in the car's confined space. The only way out was to leave him at home, in the back yard, and tell one of the neighbours that I'd be out for half an hour. He preferred to be left alone and couldn't come to harm unless someone left the gate open. If that happened while I was away and nobody noticed, there was no telling where he might finish up.

My days were almost intolerably lonely without my husband. It was three weeks before I received a letter from him. Also, there was some confusion in Australia over the exact address of the Tokyo Institute of Criminology. The Department of External Affairs didn't know, the State Government didn't know, and when I phoned the Japanese Consul I was told that there was no such address as the one David had given me. In the end I tracked down a former scholar from the Institute who had returned to Australia. He assured me that I did have the correct address, and I would eventually get my letters: it was just that mail deliveries in Japan were sometimes a bit slow.

When finally, to my relief, they did begin to arrive, dozens of them, I discovered that David had been wondering why I had not written to him. We had both written daily, and we received each other's letters in batches of six or seven.

All the time my husband was away little David kept to his usual patterns of behaviour, jumping and shouting most of the night. I kept slipping knock-out drops into his food, but, as before, they only made him drunk and he fell over. He would remain highly active until the second before he fell asleep—about 4 a.m. now—when he would suddenly drop to the floor as it were in mid-flight and sleep solidly for about four hours. Sometimes I carried him in to his bed when he fell asleep; at other times, depending on how exhausted I was, I just left him where he fell and covered him with his blankets and placed a pillow under his head. If anything, he was more active while his father was away. He could keep on with his purposeless, repetitive activity for hours: humming snatches of the same tune while he jumped on one foot, twirling a piece of string or swaying back and forth. One night, when a team of Russian dancers was performing on television, he came crashing into the room in leaps and bounds, and for the full hour of the session whirled and sprang high into the air. Fiery dances on television still stimulate him, and he keeps laughing and dancing long after they are finished.

While my husband was away I became so exhausted that I ended up taking little David's knock-out drops myself and sleeping peacefully through his wild nocturnal gaiety. That may sound irresponsible, but I was desperate, and before I took the drops I did lock all the doors and windows so that David couldn't escape.

I took him out in the car as much as I could during the day, thinking this might make him tired. It never did. Driving a car with little David in the back was not so simple as it may sound. He was fascinated with my hair, and while I drove he would pull the pins out of my hair and throw them out the window, then toss my hair like a salad. Sometimes he would lie back and put his feet in my hair. By the time I arrived at my destination I looked like Phyllis Diller. I temporarily solved this problem by giving him a mop to play with as we drove.

David attended the Children's Hospital once a week. Before I learned to drive, the Red Cross bus used to pick us up, along with some spastic children. David learned to recognize some of the spastic children and after a while he began to copy their limited movements. Whereas previously he had got out of the bus unaided, he now lay down in an awkward position and waited to be lifted out like the other children.

Another mother of an autistic child told me that she had had the same problem. Placed in a day centre for a while, her son regressed to the same level of movement as the spastic children.

During David's absence I had been working on a small book of short stories, which I realised were rather unusual. Though written in simple form, they were about children involved in extremely complex human relationships. I wanted to talk to someone accustomed to submitting manuscripts to publishers. I knew that there was a ready market for children's books, but I wanted to write books about children for adults to read.

Alan Marshall, the author, lives not far from my home in Ringwood so I phoned and asked him if he could spare some time to talk to me. He agreed to see me and said that he would be happy to meet David, well behaved or not.

The drive through the bush roads was uneventful, with David sitting quietly beside me. He seemed detached, at peace with the world for once. A friend of mine once said that David reminded her of the Midwich cuckoos and that looking into his eyes was like looking into two unfathomable pools of cold water. I had to admit that sometimes his eyes did look sightless. Today he didn't seem to be seeing anything, just looking.

When we reached the house I didn't hurry David, but let him dawdle behind me while I walked down the drive to the small bungalow among the tall trees. Alan Marshall greeted me from the doorway of his sanctuary. He stands with the aid of crutches. One of his legs is missing; he has been crippled since childhood.

That day he was alive with ideas and plans for new stories. He was in the middle of writing his Australian fairy story for children, *Whispering in the Wind*. In this book the hero is searching for a fairy princess. He has many exciting adventures, but travels in peace and learns the secret of never making enemies.

54

Alan's sister, Louise McConnell, had just written a children's story-book, *Platypus Joe*, and it was about to be published. No mean feat when you consider that Louise is seventy-eight years young.

Talking to Alan, an hour passed like five minutes. Here was a thinking man, easy to talk to, easy to listen to. I gathered hints on story-writing; he shared his knowledge without hesitation. He told me something of his travels and showed me some of his treasures. Among them was a collection of beautifully marked stones, a piece of ancient delicately carved jade, and on a table in the corner of the room he kept a pair of worn inner soles from an old pair of shoes he had found on one of his bush journeys.

At first David was too timid to come inside. But, after spending a little time standing in the sunshine in the doorway, he walked into the room and made straight for a couch in the corner. He lay on his back with his hands behind his head and stared up at the ceiling. He didn't seem to be aware of anything or anybody and was strangely quiet.

Alan told me he thought I should be able to find a publisher for my stories, but added that I should probably have to add some explanations if I wanted to reach a wide audience. "But why don't you write a book about little David?" he asked. "That should interest everyone." And I couldn't think why it hadn't occurred to me before.

When it was time to leave I called to David, not knowing what to expect of him. He rose obediently from the couch and walked towards me.

Alan stood up and leant against his desk near the door. David paused as he reached him and, with a solemn face, stretched out his hand and touched him gently on the knee. Then he looked up and I saw concern in his eyes. Alan saw it, too. David had tried to make contact with him.

While David and I walked down the shady path away from the bungalow, Alan watched from his doorway. I took my son's hand and felt a new confidence. He had behaved so beautifully. I had never known him show respect before. How much had he understood?

"Remember this day," I told David. "Today we spoke to a great man of courage."

5

THE FIRST TIME I SAW ANOTHER AUTISTIC CHILD I COULD HARDLY believe my eyes. He was like little David and yet he wasn't. His name was Richard, and I met him with his mother in the waiting-room of the Children's Hospital. His mother and I often met after that, and at one stage our children were in the same therapy group.

Richard and David behaved similarly in that they ignored each other and engaged in repetitive activities. The first day we met, Richard kept placing all the magazines from the waiting-room table on the floor and David kept running away. Richard, preoccupied and anxious, whimpered from time to time.

Later I visited Richard at his home, leaving David in the car with a small dish of water, knowing that this would keep him occupied for an hour at least.

To my surprise, Richard approached me without shyness. He sat on my lap and made me read to him from a small picture-book. He was only three years old at the time, but could recognize many letters and words. He also recognized pictures of animals, and could play chords on the piano. He kept peering down my throat when I spoke, and he put his fingers in my mouth trying to work out where the sound came from. He was intensely curious about me. There was an urgency in his manner, a tenseness, a determination to make

This is how David first began to play on the swing. It took him a long time to learn to back onto it. Here he is lost in thought, unaware of the photographer's presence. Ian Brown of the Melbourne *Herald* took this photograph and the next two while David's father was in Tokyo.

David is unaware of the photographer, but is losing his temper because the water is not splashing high enough. Soon after the photograph was taken he began hitting his head on the cement because the water was the wrong height in the bucket, but he fought me when I tried to fill it.

me repeat words and letters over and over. He was much more alert than David, who seemed quite dreamy by comparison. Yet they were alike in that neither could leave one activity once he became engaged in it and they each resisted change, each clung to ceremonies. Richard's mother, Jane, had to sing a particular song by Flanders and Swann every time he drank his milk. The song had to start when he began to drink and finish with the last drop. With his second cup of milk the song had to be sung slower because he couldn't drink it as quickly as the first. Sometimes Jane had to make the song last about twenty minutes. If anything went wrong with the timing—the song finishing before the drink, or the drink before the song—Richard became most distressed. Like David, he wanted things done the same way each day. Though he seemed extremely intelligent in some ways, far more capable and intent on learning than the usual three-year-old, he was unable to adapt; there was something inflexible about him.

Jane was extremely capable at handling him, and his elder sisters were also very helpful, but the whole family obviously felt the strain of living with such a demanding, exhausting little fellow. He had the same intolerant disposition as David, and he seemed to have the same immature nervous system.

I had the feeling that Richard didn't know what I was, that to him I was a thing to be investigated. I remember thinking at the time that neither he nor David knew they were people, knew what they were.

Jane told me that Richard had a highly developed sense of humour about other people's mishaps. He thought it extremely funny when anyone fell over or bumped into things.

Another autistic boy I visited about this time was unhappy whenever a member of his family got up from the couch in the sun-room. In this room he felt secure only when all the family sat on the couch in a row. He didn't like them moving about the room. The day I visited him he struggled with his mother when she stood up to make a cup of tea. He fought to keep her sitting on the couch.

He was a master at escaping from the house, and when he did get out there was no stopping him. He could manipulate the most difficult locks and had even been known to have a

E

go at removing a door from its hinges. He was most intelligent with tools, and could unscrew and hammer and do anything else necessary to get him where he wanted to go. His mother, a very feminine and pretty girl, looked most incongruous walking round the house with a great clanking mass of keys hanging on her belt. She was the last person you could imagine playing jailer.

When we sat down to drink our morning tea the little escaper sat politely with us and went through a ceremony of his own. He didn't spill a drop of his tea, used up all the sugar in his own bowl, and poured in all the milk from his own small jug. He insisted on having his own sugar and milk containers filled so that they could be emptied into his cup without spilling anything.

This little boy made an effort at playing with David. He lay on the floor and kicked his heels with excitement when David approached him, but David, none too friendly, kept his distance.

He was a handsome child and looked completely normal. But although he understood a lot of what was said to him he did not speak. One day his mother, missing her keys, asked the child if he had taken them. He went off, and returned later with another set of keys—one that had been lost years before. He must have remembered from way back.

Many doctors are hesitant about diagnosing children as autistic. This is understandable, for certain ways of behaving that might remind one of a child who is said to be autistic could be symptomatic of any one of a group of disorders.

From the many autistic children and mothers of autistic children that I've met, it is obvious that no two such children are exactly alike in behaviour or development. The mothers, also, have a wide range of theories about what contributed to the condition of the children. One boy was badly scalded at the age of two, and his development seemed to his mother to be affected from that time. Some mothers noticed strange behaviour in their babies from birth; others detected nothing unusual until the second or third year. Some underwent difficult pregnancies and confinements; others say they had the least worrying pregnancies and most straightforward confinements.

Benjy, a healthy-looking, placid child with beautiful eyes, doesn't speak but understands some speech. He has a mania for double garage doors and never stops looking for them. Even when the family is on an outing, a picnic or the like, if Benjy takes off suddenly his mother knows that there must be a set of double garage doors somewhere in the area. He never jams his fingers in these doors and is expert at opening and shutting them.

Another little boy I met has an insatiable interest in golf balls. This doesn't seem too bad until you see him unravel one and then start looking for another. His mother says it's an expensive pastime. This boy, too, is handsome, and has a very gentle nature.

One lad stacks chairs all over the house. When he has stacked every chair to his satisfaction, he finds some wood, hammer and nails, and tries to force his father to make more chairs.

John is five years old and has a younger brother who is greatly interested in him and takes care of him. His mother was told that John sustained brain damage at birth. As a baby, he cried without let-up, was impossible to handle and would not be eased into any sort of routine. He had a huge appetite. He was born slightly premature and his mother detected something different in him from the start.

He looked normal, seemed to develop normally—sat up, teethed, and walked on time—but from eighteen months to three years of age he went into ferocious tantrums. People kept remarking that he looked extremely intelligent, but his mother noticed that he laughed at sounds and not at the sight of things, that he found pleasure in touching different surfaces rather than in looking at things. As he grew older it became obvious that his manual dexterity was poor. Sometimes he went through periods of extreme restlessness, running back and forth aimlessly.

He has his own way of looking at things; he notices them one at a time. Mountains worry him. He picks out one tree in the garden and watches it grow. When the branches begin to sprout he says, "There is a big tree with a lot of sticks on it."

When the leaves form he says, "There are flowers on the sticks." Although he finds it difficult to grasp the abstract and his concentration in general is not as good as other children, he has a wonderful memory. He memorizes books by heart without effort. He is good at figures. He speaks well. He can read. He looks at a word sideways, squinting at it, then reads the word without difficulty. He can read words that other five-year-olds would not be able to master.

Sometimes he doesn't see things as a whole. For instance, he is only interested in certain parts of toys. Sometimes he will use the wheels of a toy and disregard the rest of it. He finds it hard to distinguish between fact and fantasy. He attends normal school, but has many problems with normal children. He shows a preference for older children and wants to join in their games. He likes chasing games, and won't stop when the other children are tired of the game; he keeps following them round and nagging at them to play with him. Yet he is often bewildered in a group at first, and if he is not familiar with the children will never make a move to get to know them.

He is a perfectionist and gets upset if he can't do things properly. He has insight into his own deficiencies, and has to be constantly reassured. He knows that other children can do some things better than he can, and he worries over it. A most anxious child, he blushes easily. He dislikes some people's faces and often laughs at other people's discomfort. He follows his father about the house, and strives constantly to be like him.

His little brother, who tries to take care of him, shows great concern when he is distressed. Sometimes he says, "What's the matter, John darling?" and John leans on him.

Children at school tease John and he is aware of it. At school he sometimes breaks down and goes to pieces. At such times he begs the teacher not to send him home because it would make him feel ashamed. But occasionally he reverts to extremely infantile behaviour and has to go home because the teacher can't manage him. He is too vulnerable to be able to cope with the rough-and-tumble of normal children. He looks forward to birthday parties and outings, but can never stand up to the actual function without becoming distressed.

He loathes wind instruments, the sound of which completely unnerves him. One day at school a child kept playing a mouth organ, and John couldn't stand it. Nevertheless he can sing well, memorizes lots of songs, and loves to join in choruses.

His mother took ages to toilet train him. She painstakingly explained it to him, over and over. He grasped the idea, but would only use the toilet at home. So his mother had to start all over again, trying to get it through to him that he was allowed to use any toilet anywhere. The message got through. One day while waiting to be served in a plumber's shop his mother was horrified to find him exhibiting his skill in the shop's window display.

Mark is nine years old, and his mother and I have become friends. It's easy to find Nan's house: it's the one with the broken window. Mark is a walker. He can think of nothing else. When Nan locks all the doors of the house he walks through the windows. At one time she owned a small shop, and nearly went out of her mind trying to serve customers and keep track of Mark. He broke the soft-drink bottles and ate lollies. He roamed the house at night, and nobody could get any sleep. He didn't know the difference between night and day. One day a customer came into the shop, bought a soft drink, and drove off in a van. When he arrived at the next town, twenty miles away, guess who leapt out of the back of the van and ran off?

When Nan and her husband missed Mark they phoned the police. Her husband set off in his car with some volunteers to organize a search party. Nan ran down to the police station to wait for news and was just in time to hear an officer on the phone saying, "A naked boy down in the coal bins at the railway siding?"

"That's my boy," Nan cried.

"They can't catch him," the officer told Nan as he hung up.

Nan's husband being off in the bush somewhere, and Nan being unable to leave the shop unattended for long, the policeman had to catch Mark alone. Knowing that Mark would jump out of the police car, he brought him home in the back of the black maria. They never did find his clothes.

When Mark was very small he had been fitted with a hearing-aid because everybody thought he was deaf. It was years before they realized that he could hear quite well, but was simply not interested in anything they had to say.

He was a keen collector of windscreen wipers off cars—an expensive hobby that cost Nan many customers.

One day Nan and Charles decided to have a family photograph taken. Though warned about Mark's walking, the photographer couldn't appreciate the problem until he saw the child in action. Mark kept walking in and out of the studio, back and forth, round cameras, in and out of the shop, in and out of the wash-room. Eventually the rest of the family hit on the idea of grouping themselves round him every time he stopped to change course. Whenever he paused they would run up and pose round him and smile. The photographer would then click away until Mark was off again. The photographs weren't too bad, considering the circumstances and their strange assortment of backgrounds.

Mark's younger brother had adjusted to his lot and knew all the ins and outs of living with an autistic relative. He and my daughter Ellen often talked things over and compared notes, commiserating with each other and sharing some of the funny experiences they had undergone. One day I heard Billy laughing at what Ellen was telling him about Double Holland. He could appreciate the need for a Double Holland when you had an autistic brother. By the time Ellen became friendly with Billy a new couple were living in Double Holland. Their names were Mr and Mrs Slubar. Mrs Slubar was large and plump and jolly and had beautiful long blonde hair. She wore large picture hats with red flowers over the crown. Her dresses were long and flowing, with tier after tier of rich pink lace. She had lots of pretty jewellery all over her arms and dangling from her neck. She wore high-heeled satin shoes, and her black velvet handbag was full of money and jewels and lovely things to eat. Mr and Mrs Slubar looked after Audie, the handsome prince of Double Holland. Mrs Slubar, a superb cook, spent hours in the palace kitchen cooking rissoles for Prince Audie. Mr Slubar was a very nice fellow who spent his days pottering round the palace, mending the roof, cleaning out the guttering, and feeding the chooks. Whenever a royal ball was held in the palace he put on his beautiful mauve velvet jacket and his deep-purple dancing shoes with the diamond buckles. He was the fanciest dancer in the whole of Double Holland. Sometimes he even outdanced the handsome prince. But the prince didn't mind when other people danced better than he did; he was happy to let them take the floor while he drank his milk and ate his rissoles.

Ellen was thrilled when I got my driving licence and kept making plans for outings and excursions which, because of little David, I couldn't keep up with. One hot Saturday afternoon, taking my courage in both hands, I promised to take her swimming. Little David looked to be in a good mood, but I knew from experience that his pleasant expression and gay little smile might not last.

The local swimming-pool was about four miles from our home. When we arrived it took me a few minutes to get David out of the car and about thirty to get him through the turnstile. After guiding him to the smallest of the three pools without much effort, I began to feel optimistic. He settled down beside the wading-pool quite happily, humming a tune as he splashed the clear water onto the concrete at the pool's edge. Ellen ran off and jumped into a larger pool. She knew that the way to get the best out of David was to leave him alone.

He was all right until some other children came over to him to see what he was doing. I don't think he was aware of their presence at all until they drew near him. Then he splashed harder and made heavy going of his tune. When, in their efforts to get a closer look at his activities, they tramped on his water patterns on the cement near the corner of the pool, he became more and more anxious and uneasy. He grizzled and splashed the water higher and higher. I tried to explain to the children that they should stay away from him, but they were too young to understand. His behaviour interested them and they didn't know what I was talking about. They crowded about him. One child bent down to look right into his face. David splashed him and tried to splash the other children's feet. One child splashed back. David screamed and tried to push the children's feet away with his hands. They trod on his fingers. Then he began to panic. He ran round in circles, fell down, and began thumping his head on the cement. His face began to swell, and his rash came up. I put my hands between his head and the cement in an effort to protect him, but I wasn't strong enough to restrain him. I dragged him to the grass, but he kept breaking away from me.

I called to Ellen, and she came running and grabbed the towels and beach bag and tried to help me get David towards the turnstile. People stood round and stared in astonishment while we battled our way to the exit. Half-way through the turnstile we became wedged. David clung to the rungs and we had to prize his hands loose. By this time he was completely lost. He was hysterical and there was no reaching him. I had to get him home as quickly as possible. When he reached this stage there was nothing else to be done. The temperature was well over ninety degrees and he was red as a beetroot, his head swollen and bruised. He badly needed some liquid, but he wouldn't drink unless he was lying on his bed at home.

Poor Ellen! She was bitterly disappointed at having to cut short her swim, and she was very worried about David.

When I arrived home, with David still hysterical, my elder son Roley was waiting. He had been in an Air Force hospital for some weeks with kidney trouble and was very depressed. He had been sent home unexpectedly on compassionate leave.

I phoned our doctor. During the fracas I had sprained my wrist and had a large gash on my hand where David had bitten me. Though his face looked a mess, he had suffered no serious damage, only bruises.

That night I couldn't sleep. I was trembling with exhaustion, too pent up to relax. David was hopping up and down the hall, humming disjointed tunes, all set for yet another night of intensified, futile, repetitive activity. I stood by the open window and looked out into the cool darkness and tried to think.

How could I go on? How could I face a lifetime of staring faces every time I took David out? The embarrassment was already hard for Ellen to take. What sort of a future was there for her with such a child in the family?

I began to think of institutions. The State Mental Health Authority had many children like David in their care, but they had a long waiting-list and could take only the most desperate cases. I wondered how desperate a mother had to be before Mental Health would take her child. Then I shrank from the thought. I knew that the institutions were over-crowded. How would they handle David's rash? How miserable he would be in a strange place with a lot of other lost children! I wondered whether he would be in physical and emotional pain for the rest of his life. There was so much I didn't know. I was tired of asking questions that had no answers. I was too tired to wonder any more, too numb to think.

That day my little boy had behaved like a savage animal. He had clawed at me, screaming and kicking. He had ripped a piece of flesh out of my hand and scratched my arms. He had turned on me as though I were his enemy, as though he were terrified of me. I knew he had been panic-stricken and I knew that I had not been able to reach him. Not being able to communicate with him had frightened me. How could I manage to look after him if he continued to deteriorate at this rate? He was now nearly five, and seemed to be getting more unreachable as he grew older. What would happen when he became too strong for me to control? He would have to be controlled by someone stronger. I thought of an older David, drugged, in a strait-jacket, screaming and fighting to be free. I thought of how much of his few years had been spent in pain. So much misery in his short life already. Watching David suffer was the hardest thing I have ever had to endure. I felt utterly defeated. I wanted to ask my husband to come home from Tokyo. I didn't want to face any more lonely nights without him. I knew that if I wrote he would come home on the next plane. But how many chances had he missed already because of me? Perhaps he would be better off without me. I wished I were dead. But I couldn't leave little David to suffer alone. He really needed me, and so did the rest of my family. I was thinking nonsense and I knew it. Somehow I just had to carry on.

I started as the phone rang.

It was my friend Rosemary Kiely, a freelance journalist. I

65

had shortly before shown her a story I had written on the theme of non-communication. She had passed it on to her husband, a sub-editor on the Melbourne *Herald*, who liked it and wanted to use it as the basis of an article about the problems of autism. They suggested that I allow myself to be identified with the article and use little David's name.

I said I'd have to think about it. My husband dislikes publicity, and as a public servant is not encouraged to seek it. It would be a lot to ask him to allow his son to be the centre of a newspaper article. (At this time very few people knew about little David.) On the other hand, it was a wonderful opportunity to get publicity for autism.

An association had lately been formed in an effort to help autistic children, of whom there were thought to be about three hundred in Victoria, and their parents. It was eventually registered under the Hospitals and Charities Act as the Victorian Autistic Children's Association. At the inaugural meeting I met Perle Treweek, the girl behind the move to get parents organized. Perle was a tireless worker and spent every available minute raising funds, giving talks, and writing articles. I don't think we would have an association in Victoria yet if Perle had not started the action.

I was cautious at first about getting publicity for autism. I felt that we didn't know enough about the condition and I was not too sure where we were heading. I knew some parents wanted to go flat out and raise funds, but I wasn't sure what we should do with the money when we got it. Some parents wanted to set up a centre immediately; others wanted to find out more about the children's problems. There were discussions over the type of qualifications we should require in a teacher, and so on.

One problem with this disturbance is that parents of the children often don't see the full extent of their children's disabilities. I knew that once the parents got to comparing notes some would be upset if their children didn't progress as quickly as others. There seemed to be a tendency to regard autism as one complaint and to expect the same type of results with each child. I felt by this time that many types of disturbance were labelled autism. There was no proof that any forms of treatment or methods of handling the children

66

could be termed the "right" ones. So much was not known, everything was still in an experimental stage. I could see that some parents would be terribly disappointed in their search for cures that didn't exist, and others would expect performances that their children couldn't give.

Having read that autistic children needed one teacher to each child, I was worried about the enormous cost of keeping such a centre operating. But I was also aware that each so-called autistic child had bewildered and unhappy parents. So I decided to plunge in. Without publicity, people at large would never know that such a condition as autism existed; and I thought it would be good for parents of autistic children to know that they were not alone with their problems.

I phoned John Kiely and told him he could go ahead, provided he questioned a psychiatrist about autism. I didn't want to be regarded as the spokeswoman for this complex illness.

John got the story into shape, changing the title from "The Shy Little Boy" to "The Small Outsider". When it was published many people phoned me, wanting to know more about the condition. Most of them had never heard of it, and some could hardly believe it existed.

Some of the parents in the association were anxious to start a centre as soon as possible; others wanted to wait until a professional advisory body was set up to help select staff and assess children. Eventually two energetic mothers set up the first centre in Victoria devoted solely to the care of autistic children. Some parents were worried because the teacher, though trained for primary-school work, did not have the special qualifications they considered desirable. But the teacher proved herself extremely capable, with a natural feeling for the children's problems. The centre's eight vacancies were soon filled. The parents of these eight children were delighted with their centre and it was quite obvious that they benefited greatly from being relieved of a part of their heavy burden. As one exhausted mother put it, "This teacher may not have the special teacher certificate for dealing with handicapped children, but then neither have I, and I've been coping for nine years."

One remarkable feature of the centre was the amount of voluntary help its organizers got. They sent out calls for people who would work with the children in rosters, helping to mind them under the principal's supervision. Most of these women had school-age or grown-up children, and could spare a few hours a week or fortnight to stay at the centre trying to gain the confidence of the children or just keeping them out of harm's way generally. They were remarkable women; and over the years many of them have formed strong attachments to the children they work with. Some of them—teachers, nurses and the like before marriage—have taken up courses to help them understand and guide the children more effectively.

Another aid in operating a centre with so few parents has been the number of people who have volunteered to serve on committees, help raise funds, and do administrative work.

Later a second centre was opened by hard-working parents and voluntary helpers, and has progressed splendidly. The enthusiastic principal has the support of two other professional staff members plus women volunteers. Both centres were granted Government subsidies.

I think that John Brett, the association's president, can now be confident that, after his years of patient work and guidance, the association is well launched. Some of the parents now want to have buildings of their own, as the church halls now being used as temporary accommodation for the centres are not always suitable in all ways for the teaching needs. A building fund has been started.

6

ONE DAY A LETTER ARRIVED FROM MY MOTHER SAYING THAT she was coming to keep me company while my husband was in Tokyo.

Only one thing worried me about this otherwise wonderful news—Grandmother's clock. Mother was sure to ask about it when she arrived. It had been in her family for generations and she had given it to me some time before, in the belief that I'd like to have it. I did, too. But unfortunately, so did little David.

Arriving at a time when he was particularly blank and showed little interest in anything, it seemed to bring him to life. He spent hours looking at it, and its chimes pleased him. He used to do a little ceremonial dance up and down the room in front of it several times each day, and when it chimed he would stand and stare, spellbound. Gradually he gathered sufficient courage to touch it. One day I saw him climb up on a kitchen stool to get better acquainted with it. I was delighted to see him showing such initiative until I realized the implications. From then on the clock knew no peace. No matter where I put it he found it. He learned to open its glass door and move its hands round and round till it became all mixed up and started chiming the hour on the half-hour. Once, at midnight, it struck nineteen.

The watchmaker I took it to was obviously a lover of fine

old clocks. He examined it gently. "Someone's been tinkering with this," he said. "It's in a terrible mess. I'll have to adjust everything. It will take at least three weeks."

In a way I was relieved. In that time, I thought, David would forget the clock. I should have known better. When I brought it home again I placed it on a different shelf, thinking he wouldn't notice it. But it wasn't long before he had found it and spun the hands round so much that it stopped chiming altogether. Now it just made strange whirring noises and occasionally twanged.

The watchmaker could hardly believe it when I went back and shamefacedly slid the clock over the counter.

"What vandal could have done such a thing?" he wanted to know. "It's unbelievable that anybody could manhandle such a fine old piece of craftsmanship. This clock will take months to settle down again. It may never recover."

I bought a brightly coloured alarm-clock for David, but when I gave it to him he looked at me coldly, as though I had done him an injury, and dropped it nonchalantly on the floor. He never looked at it again.

When Grandmother's clock had been mended again, I hid it in a cupboard behind the kitchen door.

The next time I returned it to the watchmaker, he couldn't bring himself to speak to me. He just took a deep breath and stood gazing at it.

David had found it one night while we were all asleep, had ripped off the glass door and thrown it away, and twisted the hands round and round each other. I woke to hear the clock throwing some sort of convulsion as it struggled to untangle its hands. It whined and spluttered startlingly, then gave a loud clang and fell silent.

The watchmaker gave up and so did I. I locked the clock in a wardrobe and hid the key. But David still managed to find it occasionally, and each time he did he ripped something off it.

He was most interested in my mother. He kept climbing over her and sliding down off her lap as though she were a slippery-dip. She loved him, but couldn't stand up to his treatment of her. She was nearing seventy, and there was a limit to what she could stand from an enthusiastic five-year-old. It was useless trying to convince him that people feel

70

pain. Mother spent most of her time shut up in the dining-room with her crochet work where David couldn't get to her. Every time he caught a glimpse of her he tried to get to her. He loved her in his own limited way, but was too rough. When I took her for a drive with the children he kept trying to jump up and down in her lap. He responded to her like a year-old baby, demanding the same physical support and romping.

In spite of his acceptance of her, however, he wouldn't allow her to kiss him. He had never allowed anyone to kiss him.

It was Eric Benjamin, a colleague of my husband's, who suggested the mirror. Eric has a rare gift of understanding, and I have seen him get through to the most unreachable people. He told me how he had helped a deaf boy who was afraid of people by confronting him as often as possible with his own image in a mirror. The boy loosened up by recognizing his own face and realizing that he had control over his features. Eric suggested that we place a full-length mirror in the nursery and stand with David so that he could come to see that he was like us. Every day I used to stand in front of this mirror with David and point to myself and say, "Mummy", and then point to him and say, "David." It was a wonderful suggestion, because although his interest came and went, he often talked to his own image in his own language and enjoyed communicating with himself. I think that as his awareness of the world around him increased, so did his awareness of himself. Sometimes he would lean against the wall next to the mirror and slowly peep at his reflection by turning his head at an angle. Sometimes he would simply stand motionless in front of his image with a satisfied look on his face.

I've heard it said that while some autistic children love mirrors, others fear them, and I agree that caution ought to be exercised about introducing them to each other. At the start I was the only person whose reflection David saw beside himself. I don't think it would have done him good if he had seen a lot of people; he might have become frightened or confused. I introduced him to the mirror very gently. I let him stay in front of it only as long as he wanted to; I never tried to force him. Although there were many times when he looked blank and paid no attention to the mirror, he did get something out of the experience.

One day when Mother was about to go out shopping she tried as usual to kiss David, and he ran away and hid his face. A little while later I found him in the nursery kissing his own image in the mirror. After that he used to commune with people's faces on television, sitting very close to the screen and laughing at them.

David's encounter with the mirror also encouraged me because I was sure that his vision was not normal, and I thought that studying the reflections might help him. I have read that some autistic children have distorted vision; their sight messages don't get through the way they should. David often studied objects out of the corner of his eye and he sometimes became distressed when he saw small children moving about. I think he felt uneasy in the presence of smaller children because they moved about below his eye level. He seemed to see only from certain angles. He also saw some shapes and colours better than others. Against certain backgrounds, some colours didn't seem to register with him at all. Fast-moving shapes against contrasting backgrounds attracted his attention. If he was interested in an object he spun or waved it back and forth. I suspected that he did not see people very clearly. Human beings are indefinite in colour, and against a pale background they must have looked blurry to him. It seemed to me that when someone was sitting in a chair David was not too sure where the person ended and the chair began. Sometimes when he wanted me to do something for him he would make a grab at my hand, miss, and grab the arm of the chair instead. After a few tugs at the chair he would realize his mistake and feel along the arm of the chair till he reached my hand. He could tell my hand by the feel of it. I think his vision and perceptiveness have changed from time to time.

His hearing, too, seemed to be distorted. He did not hear some sounds and seemed to register high-pitched sounds better than low-pitched ones. He did not appear to hear thunder at all.

In trying to communicate with him I have relied more on touch than on speech. Sometimes speech reaches him, but if it doesn't and I want him to come to me, I go to him and ease him off in the direction I want him to go. Sometimes I have to stand behind him and lean over and guide him with my hands under his arms. Sometimes he responds to his name, but not always. He himself finds touch very useful. He touches every surface, going more by the feel of objects than the sight of them. Given his limited perception, this is understandable. He can get a lot of information out of touching an object. He shows more interest in objects with uneven surfaces than those with smooth surfaces.

His interest in Mother was strange. He hadn't seen her since babyhood, but he became quite excited when he saw her again on her visit to us. He is full of surprises; I never know what he is going to do when he meets a new person. But his enjoyment of Mother's company was obvious. It seems most unlikely that he remembered her from our visit to Toowoomba, but he certainly acted as though he did.

The night Mother was leaving, while I was driving her to the station, she asked the question I had hoped she wouldn't: "What ever happened to Grandmother's clock?"

It was a hard thing to explain, but not as hard as it would have been before Mother had spent a few weeks in the same house as little David. You have to actually live with him in order to understand some things.

When my husband returned from Tokyo he noticed a big improvement in little David. He found him far more receptive than he had been three months earlier. It was true. David appeared to be emerging gradually from his autistic state. Without any prompting he was slowly becoming more aware of the world about him. Sometimes when he experienced something new he was frightened, but he was responding more and more to things he had not previously noticed.

One surprising day he recognized food for the first time. I was chopping the leaves off a stick of celery to put in a stew when he snatched it out of my hand, stood looking at it for a while, then made little muttering sounds to himself as he waved it about and studied it from different angles. Then he walked off up the hall, chewing it. A few minutes later he came back and ate a piece of potato peel. Then he swept a

F.

piece of raw steak into his mouth and chewed it enthusiastically.

From then he tasted everything he ran across. Within a few months he had eaten his way through an incredible number of unlikely substances. He ate the cuffs off his shirts, took off his socks and chewed them up into tiny shreds, and within six weeks munched his way through an entire bedspread. He was like a moth. He chewed dozens of holes in our blankets and nibbled the bottoms off all the clothes hanging on the line. He worried the pompoms on slippers, and chewed through the cords of blinds. He became fascinated with mashed potatoes, and if I left them unattended he trampled in them, laughing at the sheer fun of it, pleased at the way they squeezed up between his toes.

He not only felt new things with his mouth now, but kept taking off his clothes and feeling them with the rest of his body. If he saw a new piece of material he would strip off and roll in it on the floor. He threw food on the floor and trampled on it or rolled in it. Once, for about a month, he got the idea of placing pieces of meat or vegetables on his bottom. Every time they fell off he would stop, pick them up and stick them back again with a slapping noise. Fortunately, the novelty wore off.

A few weeks after his awareness of food developed, David, who was five years old at the time, began to concentrate on raw meat. He chewed it, threw it around, worried it. He got down on the floor and frolicked with it. He crawled up and down the hall with it in his mouth like a puppy, and chewed it with his head low to the floor. If you had caught your first sight of him at this stage you might have thought he had been reared by dogs. In fact he has never liked dogs, and had certainly never seen them eat, so he was not copying them. He reminded me of descriptions I had read of the feral children of India who were thought to have been reared by wolves. The story of these children has never made much sense to me. I think it likely that they were children like David, possibly abandoned by their parents.

This wild-dog stage passed fairly quickly, and for the first time he started taking an interest in meals on plates. After a while he would allow me to place spoonfuls of food in his mouth, at first accepting anything, and later discriminating as he discovered that there were certain foods he didn't like.

Eating was now so exciting to him that he filled his days putting things in his mouth. All day long he munched away at anything and everything in the yard. He filled his mouth with gravel daily and must have swallowed at least some of the earth and stones. He was clumsy and couldn't spit things out. If something interested him he would automatically place it in his mouth to investigate it further. Then he couldn't work out how to get rid of it.

He foraged in the garbage can, holding the lid upturned in one hand like an *hors d'œuvre* tray, salvaging items of interesting texture, colour, and smell, arranging them on the lid, and tasting each one in turn, like a connoisseur. Several times he filled his mouth with bottle-tops, and on one occasion with broken glass. He ate plants from the garden, and once filled his mouth with rusty nails. We had to go over the yard with a fine rake to remove all dangerous rocks, sticks, and debris. He chewed up snails, beetles, and grubs. When there was nothing left in the yard but dirt, he filled his mouth with that. Getting him to spit it out when it was time to have lunch was impossible; he usually finished up swallowing it along with his food. He got lots of tummy upsets, but on the whole he didn't seem to mind. Once an ant bit him in the mouth, but this didn't stop him eating ants when he could catch them.

The therapist at the Children's Hospital suggested that I keep his mouth full of Gran Bits, a breakfast cereal. This worked. All through the day, at intervals of about twenty minutes or so, I would fill his mouth with cereal as full as it would go. He would potter round, happily sucking on the granules till they were absorbed; then I had to be ready with the refill. He still managed to slip in the odd mouthful of dirt and pebbles, but on the whole the granules were a great success. He loved them.

Strangely enough, whereas he had previously shown interest only in bland, smooth foods, he now developed a passion for rough, crisp things and refused anything even vaguely mushy. Taste didn't seem to interest him as much as texture. He would eat the most unspeakable substances if their texture was uneven. Every time he saw something new he felt it first with his hands, then placed it against his cheek or chest and finally put it in his mouth.

At about this time he started touching his head and feeling his hair. He also touched his ears and nose. I tried to tell him the words for nose, ears, eyes, and so on, but most times he would push me away as if I bored him.

One night he discovered that if he ate into his pillow a great mass of foam plastic came bursting out. When I discovered him he had his mouth full of the stuff, his bed was buried in it, and it was all over the room. I hadn't realized there was so much foam stuffed into one pillow. David frolicked in the mess and laughed with glee. I made a strong calico case and used the same foam to fill it. The next night, though it took him a little longer, David ate a large hole in the calico, and I had to spend another night cleaning up while he rolled on the floor and laughed. The night after that he ate huge chunks out of his mattress. From then on no cushion or pillow or mattress in the house was safe. All were eaten through or whittled away. The house looked like a popcorn factory gone wrong.

One day while David was at the height of his foam-plastic period a salesman came to the front door, and when I opened it David, who had been wallowing in a pile of foam just inside it, slithered out on a cascading billow of plastic. The astonished salesman, who was selling floor-polishers, didn't stay long at this house that was evidently full of foam plastic. As he hurried up the path he brushed busily at his suit. Foam plastic is terrible stuff to get off clothes; it sticks to everything.

During his plastic stage I simply let David have his head. After I had admitted defeat, and resigned myself to living with the stuff it wasn't so bad. I knew by then that David's obsessions don't last. This is the secret of living with him without going round the bend.

That winter David developed some severe head colds and some nights seemed to have difficulty in breathing. I suspected that his touch of asthma had returned, but I wasn't sure. Several times he was given medicine and the trouble almost cleared up, but never quite. Eventually a doctor at the Children's Hospital sent me to Casualty to see if there was a blockage in David's nose. The doctor in Casualty found it impossible to give David a thorough examination without putting him under an anaesthetic. I was frantic. So many things had gone wrong with David in the past that I was terrified of what the doctor might find.

On the morning of the examination Ellen was ill, and since my husband had to be at work early I had to get a sitter for her. Dot Cullamore obliged. She had phoned me out of the blue one day and asked if she could help me. This was just the sort of emergency that needed a girl like Dot. I knew that Ellen would be happy with Dot and this left me free to concentrate on David.

David wasn't allowed to have any food before the examination, and I had to get him to hospital at 9 a.m. By the time he was officially admitted as a patient it was 11.30. While we waited David kept stripping off his clothes, rolling on the floor, and chewing up magazines on the waiting-room table. He stole a woman's handbag and locked himself in one of the doctor's rooms. He crawled round on his hands and knees among the office staff, who kept tripping over him. He ate the pompom off his cap. When we got to his ward he was filthy and I had to wash him for the operating theatre. When the nurse came to take his temperature he drank the thermometer water while she was shaking the thermometer. He behaved like a monkey, climbing on and off beds, springing on and off tables and chairs and cupboards, shouting and laughing. I kept calling to him and trying to hold him down, but he completely ignored me.

When at last he was ready for the theatre I had to hold him down while the nurse gave him a calming injection. Before this it had all been a game. Now he became quiet and apprehensive, sitting against the wall of his cot, trembling. I tried to nurse him, but he pushed me away.

When the wardsman came to wheel him away on the trolley he suddenly turned to me and put out his arms and looked up at me with a pleading expression on his face. He had never done this in his life before. The wardsman quickly swept him onto the trolley and wheeled him down the corridor. I watched him go, a frightened, forlorn little figure in a shapeless white overall, huddled against the bar of the trolley. I felt as though my heart would break.

Since I wouldn't see David for two hours, I went downstairs and phoned my husband. He came over to the hospital and we waited in the canteen and tried to drink coffee. It was a long two hours. David's psychiatrist sat with us for a while and tried to make things easier for us.

Shortly after we returned to the ward little David was wheeled in, asleep and very pale. A large quantity of foam plastic had been found, packed tightly up his nostrils. Nothing more, no complications.

Immensely relieved, we sat down to wait till seven o'clock, when we would be able to take David home. Ellen's sitter was to leave at five o'clock, so I had to phone a neighbour and ask her to stand in. We got back to Ringwood at eight o'clock. It had been a long day.

It took David about a week to forgive us for the operation and start eating again. Although his throat seemed sore and he had difficulty swallowing, he was soon getting on with the business of exploring surfaces and eating rubbish.

After the operation he took on a new interest in everything. He became more alert, and for some weeks seemed to be trying to please us. He came when we called him, or stood around smiling, waiting to see if we wanted him for anything. I had never known him so co-operative. For some time, in my efforts to teach him to communicate with us by touch, I had been leading him round and placing his hands on things I wanted him to notice. Now he started doing the same with me. If he wanted something out of the refrigerator he would place my hand on the handle of its door. If he wanted a bath he would lead me to the bathroom and place my hand on the taps. The first time he got a message to me in this way he was so pleased with himself that he burst out laughing. He placed my hand on the knob of the back door. I opened it. He ran outside and a few minutes later came in through the front door, which was open, ran up to me, grabbed my hand, and made me open the back door again. Then, drunk with power, he repeated the performance. This time I left the back door open. He began to cry, and pushed me over to the door and forced me to close it again. When he was ready he made me

78

open it, and completed another circuit of the house. This went on for about a week before the novelty wore off.

After gaining my co-operation in this definite way he took on a new air of confidence. He began to strut through the house, stamping his heels as he walked. He swaggered round the yard, full of self-assurance. He had learned to communicate, and he was aware of it.

Nowadays he can open some of the doors himself, but every so often he still makes someone else open a door for him, just to prove to himself that he's in charge. I can see by his face when he is proud of himself.

He can feed himself now, too. He could do without his bottles altogether, but I still give him his breakfast of cereal and boiled milk and prunes through his four bottles because if he ever has to take medicine the bottles are the easiest way to get him to swallow it. Though he will usually take anything through a bottle he won't accept a new drink from a cup. He used to drink twenty bottles of food a day; now he is down to four. His twenty bottles a day had to be fed to him while he was lying on his bed. He had them four at a time, and there was a special way he had to drink them. He would sample each one in turn, and when he had tasted all four and consumed the same amount out of each bottle, he would go the rounds again, drinking the same amount again from each bottle. Whenever he had a rest he would look to see if the level of food was the same in each bottle. If one of them contained more than the rest he would drink it down to the same level as the others. Some days he would want to drink from the bottles out of order—for instance, numbers one, three, two, and four, or four, two, three, and one. The pattern he adopted at the start of any meal had to be maintained throughout.

In this eventful sixth year of his, he simply grew out of his bottles, except at breakfast, finding it more interesting to feed himself sitting at the table with the rest of the family. At first I used to tie him to his chair with a piece of ribbon, but after a few days he sat up by himself. He doesn't always sit at the table till the meal is ended; sometimes he will take a mouthful of rissoles (his top favourite dish) and run round till he has eaten them, then return for more. But he is learning all the time. Because of his continuing interest in the texture of what he eats, he cares little for spoons and forks, and still prefers to feed himself by hand.

The members of our family usually carry their own plates from the kitchen to the dining-room table, and David is no exception. He waits beside me while I prepare his rissoles, then carefully picks up his plate so as not to spill anything, swings it under his arm with a flourish and marches off to the dining-room. When he reaches the table and discovers that his dinner has disappeared and he is the only one with an empty plate, he has hysterics. Sometimes, instead of putting his plate under his arm, he swings it nonchalantly in one hand as he walks. We have to run behind him picking up rissoles so that he won't feel too victimized. He really puzzles over this problem. You can almost see his brain working on it, and I'm sure he'll get on top of it before long.

His love of rissoles goes way beyond a liking for the taste. He loves them for themselves. He collects them, and places them in little heaps for recreation. Sometimes you find them stashed away behind the kitchen door, and he usually keeps a small number in a drawer with his underwear. Whenever my overcoat has been hanging on the hallstand I might later find a rissole in one pocket of it while I'm searching for small change in a shop. Stray dogs have become interested in our house and hang round expectantly, waiting for me to sweep the floors each day. Whenever I step outside they rush me and sniff my shoes, because I usually have some part of a rissole clinging to my heels.

David also loves toilet paper, and he plays with it quite a lot. He will take it off its holder in the bathroom, hold one end, and run as fast as he can with the roll billowing out behind him. He has the greatest admiration for nicely coloured toilet paper, and gets most indignant when he sees the way other children treat it.

We recently visited a friend whose eight-year-old son, James, had displayed autistic tendencies. When he was three his mother thought him a little slow. He did not speak till he was four, and then only in isolated nouns. His mother had a good grasp of his condition and he made a remarkable recovery. The family lived in England at one time, and there James attended a Montessori school, which seems to have benefited him greatly. The Montessori system attempts to link the child's different senses so that more than one channel of learning is available. The child is provided with materials designed to stimulate and interest him through his senses of touch, sight, and hearing. By handling these he becomes aware of differences in diameter, length, shape, width, height, weight, texture, sound, and colour. He can trace with his hands sandpaper letters and figures on raised blocks and hear the appropriate phonetic sound or symbol at the same time.

At the age of eight James was attending normal school and was capable of learning at the same pace as other children. His vocabulary seemed to me better than that of the average child of his age. He had a remarkable memory and could store up much complicated information. There was something unusual, however, about his relationships with people. He could not take part in group conversations; he had to take each person away from the group in order to converse. Such peculiarities were noticeable to other children at his school.

Ellen enjoyed James's company. She is a togetherness child, and James gave her his undivided attention. He built a dam in his sand pile and filled it with water from the hose, keeping her informed on the reasons for the thickness of the walls and similar matters. She was most impressed by his knowledge.

He is a delightful little boy, but very serious, taking everything at face value. During our visit he took me by the hand, led me away from the group of people seated in the courtyard, and invited me to sit on a rock in the corner of the garden. He then spread a map on my lap and asked me to point out all the disused train lines in Victoria. I told him that I didn't know anything about disused train lines. Ignoring what I had said, he asked me to think hard and try to work out where the disused lines might be. I said I had no idea where they might be, so he started working it out on his own. He knew where all the former mining towns were and he started a long monologue on the likelihood of there being a disused train line between one such town and the next town. Every now and then he would ask me a question to which I had no answer.

Whenever I told him that I simply didn't know where the disused train lines were, he would change his approach to the question. By the time his mother rescued me he seemed to have exhausted every approach that could possibly be used to persuade me to search every nook and cranny of my mind for some tiny piece of information about disused train lines that might be lurking there without my realizing it.

Next he approached my husband, who decided to get in first and change the subject. He asked James if he liked the zoo. James countered by asking my husband if he liked ant-eaters.

My husband faltered and said that he had never given them any thought.

"Well, think about them," said James. "And while you're thinking about them, tell me whether your wife and daughter like ant-eaters."

"Well, I have never asked them," replied my husband. "But I don't think they like them much."

"Doesn't anybody like ant-eaters?" asked James.

"Well, I suppose somebody must," said my husband, looking wilted.

"Who are they?"

"I don't know," replied my husband, at his wits end.

James was silent for a moment, and then asked, "Do ants like ant-eaters?"

7

DURING THE LAST FEW YEARS I HAVE SPOKEN TO HUNDREDS OF parents of handicapped children. My telephone always seems to be ringing, and I don't mind because I like talking to people about this problem, comparing notes and exchanging questions.

Mothers often ask me how I knew for sure that there was something wrong with David so soon after birth and why I didn't have much hope for him after I first handled him. I find this hard to explain. Throughout the pregnancy I had felt that David was not right, that he had no hope before he was born. As soon as I saw him and counted his fingers and toes I was delighted; he looked so normal. But when I handled him again and tried to gain his co-operation in feeding I felt quite sure that he was very definitely damaged. Oddly enough, I have spoken to five other mothers of handicapped children who all had had the same feeling before the birth. There was no obvious reason why their children should not have been normal before birth; nevertheless the children were handicapped, and the damage had obviously occurred long before birth. I suppose some mothers simply know, somehow, when they are carrying damaged babies.

I have also had many phone calls from parents with children whom they describe as delinquent, and I am surprised that they all say much the same things as do parents of autistic children. "This child has never been easy to understand." "I just can't seem to get through to him." "Sometimes he acts as though he is deaf." "He does the same things over and over again and never learns a lesson." I wonder if these children could be suffering from some form of nerve damage. Perhaps the ones we call autistic are the ones most severely affected.

People often ask whether there are more autistic children now than there used to be. They are surprised that such a condition exists and they want to know why they have not heard about it before. I have no way of finding out whether there are more autistic children now than there used to be, but I have a feeling that there could be. To start off with, more babies survive today. Women who look like miscarrying are often prevented from doing so by injections. It is reasonable to assume that some of today's damaged children would not have survived in earlier times. Some mothers have told me that their autistic children were born prematurely. More premature babies survive today, so I suppose some autistic children in this group survive now who would not have survived in days gone by. (This does not mean that all mothers who haemorrhage during pregnancy or produce premature babies will have autistic children, but the autistic children born to this group might have been lost without modern medical care.)

Then we have present-day methods of feeding babies, and vitamin compounds and immunization. Fifty years ago the slow and difficult feeders among autistic children might not have had the same chance of survival as they have now. Before the days of antibiotics some of them could have weakened and died of infections. Even today we sometimes read in the papers of a mother with a number of very young children who loses a child through malnutrition. Once a baby becomes weak it ceases to kick up a fuss when it's hungry, and the mother, if she is very busy with other toddlers, may think it is all right because it's quiet. I wonder whether some of these children could be autistic.

Some autistic children no doubt survived in previous days. I read one account of a boy who had been placed in an institution for the deaf when he was very young. At the age of seventeen he was tested and found to have normal hearing. He had never spoken, presumably because nobody had expected him to speak. It was suggested that he could have been autistic as a child and after recovering from the autistic state had remained mute.

There is a story that Mozart and Einstein were autistic when children. I can find no evidence to support it. One theory about autistic children that doesn't ring true to me is that they are potential geniuses. I have certainly never met an autistic child whom I considered a genius in the making, but of course mine is not the final word on this and I could be wrong.

There is a famous old book called *The Wild Boy of Aveyron* by Jean-Marc-Gaspard Itard. Dr Itard, a French physician, was born in 1774 and died in 1838. His book was written about a child who was found naked, wandering in the woods making strange sounds like a wild animal. Dr Itard took this boy home with him and tried to adapt him to society. I don't know whether the boy could have been called autistic, but he behaved somewhat like an autistic child. The list of aims set out by Dr Itard in training the boy were by today's standards very good ones. To begin with, he tried "to interest the boy in social life by rendering it more pleasant than the one he was leading". He didn't get as far with the training as he had hoped (often the situation is the same today), but he set out some sound basic ideas for handling mentally handicapped children. His pupil Edward Seguin later took over Dr Itard's ideas and in 1837 opened in Paris what he called a school for idiots, where education based on the five senses was applied for the first time. In 1848 Dr Seguin went to the United States, where his theories based on the idea that education of the senses must come before education of the mind were freely adopted. In teaching children with immature nervous systems he concentrated on the principle of first trying to develop the imperfect senses.

Maria Montessori, who in 1894 was the first woman in Italy to graduate in medicine from the University of Rome, subsequently took up the study of educating defective children. She developed her teaching methods after studying the work of Dr Itard and Dr Seguin. Later she found that her methods were equally successful when applied to normal children. Her book, *The Montessori Method*, published in 1912, became world-famous. Today her ideas are sprinkled throughout education systems in most parts of the world. There are certain centres that concentrate on the Montessori Method as such, but I think all kindergartens in Australia probably follow a lot of Montessori ideas in allowing children to learn through play and giving them free choice in the selection of play materials.

People often phone to tell me that they have read about cures for autistic children in a magazine or newspaper. I am always grateful to any magazine or newspaper that runs articles on autism, because I think it needs wider and wider recognition. At the same time I think the cure angle could be misleading, since it tends to minimize the problems likely to be encountered when the apparently cured child tries to join society. Often the biggest job of all is getting society to accept the slightly odd, otherwise recovered, autistic child. "Cure" articles give the public the impression that all autistic children will become normal in all respects after treatment and so can be forgotten.

There are many traps in writing about autism. I'm constantly aware as I write that I may be proved wrong on some point or other at any time. And I know that many things I write will not be acceptable to everyone. It's a most difficult subject. I would like to see the public informed that it may not be possible for all autistic children to be turned out exactly the same as everybody else. All we can really do is try to help the child adjust to his environment sufficiently to enable him to mix with other people. I doubt if he will ever be exactly the same as people who have never had an autistic personality. Many children will still need institutional and hostel care when they grow up, no matter how much teaching and treatment they receive.

The autistic child loses a lot of ground during childhood and it seems unlikely that he can ever catch up to the extent that his strangeness will not be noticeable sometimes. Even if he is educable in the accepted sense—that is, able to attend normal school and keep up with reading, writing, and arithmetic—his behaviour could be unusual. He could find it difficult to understand other people's feelings. He could develop a good memory and be able to answer complicated questions, yet continue to maintain an interest in literature at the pre-school level and be quite intense about it. His development is sometimes uneven.

I believe that the autistic children I have met have suffered some physical damage to the brain, central nervous system, or some vital part of their mechanism related to the relaying of messages. I believe that some are so badly damaged that their progress will never be spectacular. For each one who learns to speak there will be more who don't. Even so, those without speech do tend to improve, and it is often possible to help them to live reasonably well with their families. Many learn to understand some speech, even though they don't speak themselves, and some co-operate.

I don't think it can be too strongly stressed, however, that the family of the autistic child is a family at risk. The normal children in it often suffer greatly as a result of living with a difficult child. The progress that the autistic child makes in his own home should always be measured against the side-effects he produces in his family. If the autistic child is making good progress at the expense of his normal brothers and sisters I think every effort should be made to have him placed in another environment, namely some live-in-type hostel. It is pointless to have a perfectly adjusted autistic child if the rest of his family is destroyed. And believe me, nobody can destroy a family quite like some autistic children I have seen. He knows only his needs of the moment and has great difficulty in learning that others must be considered.

If the autistic child seems strange to other people, other people seem strange to the autistic child. We at least have the advantage of knowing that he is one of us, though different in some ways, but he often doesn't know what he is and can't see himself in relation to his environment.

Even when learning to speak, some autistic children don't use the word "I". If you say, "Do you want an apple?" they reply, "Do you want on apple?" But if you ask, "Do I want an apple?" they answer, "Do you want an apple?" They change the sentence to exclude "I" because "I" is beyond their ken.

I know one young man who looks at himself through a mirror all the time and never lets go his mirror, day or night. Without it he has no identity, and he screams if he loses it. He can't *imagine* himself, he must *see* himself.

I still have trouble accepting the idea of training autistic children to refrain from their strange behaviour while we won't know what causes it.

The idea of teaching David before I find out what is actually wrong with him makes me feel like the mother of a child who limps and whose doctors can't find a physical reason for the limp. I find myself with no alternative but to train the child to stop limping by education. If I succeed I shall have cured only a symptom of his trouble, not the trouble itself. This is what we do when we stop the autistic child from indulging in his strange behaviour. Take the flicking of objects against different-coloured backgrounds. A child may have distorted vision, he flicks a pencil or some such object back and forth and looks at it out of the corner of his eye. When he begins to be trained the teachers will try to stop him from flicking the pencil. Every time they see him do it they will hold his hands and try to get him to do something else; they may have to resort to scolding or slapping. If they work long enough they will probably win and the child will stop flicking objects while they are watching him. This seems to make everybody happy except the child. He still has to live with his distorted vision, but has been forced to give up the activity that revealed his trouble to other people. If we no longer see him displaying the symptom of his illness we kid ourselves that he is cured.

Sometimes the child continues to flick the pencil through habit, after his vision has begun to improve and register more normally. In this case there is some point in trying to curtail the activity.

Moreover, we have to know that the child is capable of more meaningful activity before trying to change him. If we stop him from flicking a pencil and he starts smashing the furniture we shan't have done much good. The child seems to pass through certain developmental stages. It could be helpful if the therapist followed the trends of the child when

David, at four, still resisted all attempts to cuddle him. Here he
is easing himself away from my cheek with his arm. He is
aware of the photographer but refuses to look at him.

David, aged six, playing with his "nigh-nigh" pillow. He is aware of the photographer and smiling at him. Neil Town took this photograph and the next three.

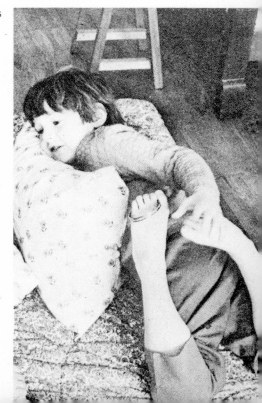

David wearing a bracelet on his foot instead of his arm.

deciding at what time to stop and start each type of new lesson. I think the teacher should work in close co-operation with a psychiatrist, one experienced in the handling of these children.

A therapist working with a child passing through a severely withdrawn phase could work for years before seeing any change. If the child suddenly appeared to catch on the therapist would naturally assume that the therapy had been worth while. But the child could merely be emerging from his withdrawn state, growing capable of more understanding at that particular phase of his development. At certain times of his life the child is more receptive to outside influences.

The child often indulges in forms of repetitive activity as a kind of hypnotic escapism. Perhaps he needs to escape sometimes.

We often read that we should try to give the autistic child a more meaningful world to live in. What we really mean is that we want to replace his world, which is meaningful to him, with one of our own design which is meaningful to us. The things he does don't make sense to us, but they may make sense to him. I realize that we can't live with him without his making some adjustment to our way of life, but I think we should tread softly when forcing him to leave his world of isolation.

Some people say that haste is essential in training the autistic child to refrain from his annoying ways, but others say you should let him take his time and he will modify much of his behaviour of his own accord. I think we should at least take some leads from him, especially since we don't really know what effect our enforced curtailing of his escapist activities has on his aggressions. In the long run stirring up too much aggression could cause more trouble than those activities gave. It doesn't matter how many skills he learns; if he continues to attack people there will be no place for him outside an institution.

Experts on autism are cropping up all over the world now like mushrooms after a warm spring shower. And when they talk of treatment they often mean different things. People practise a wide range of experiments on these children in the name of treatment. But some children do seem to improve

G

without anything unusual having been done. Some emerge from their autistic state as they get older. They just begin to see the world about them clearer as their nervous systems grow stronger.

One very "in" way of treating autistic children at present is known as operant conditioning. This is a scientific method of teaching by reward and punishment, researched painstakingly by Professor B. F. Skinner of Harvard University, who has devoted many years to its development. His work seems to be more concerned with the prediction of behaviour than the understanding of it, and he has devised some impressive methods of controlling behaviour. Many educationalists have built upon his research and worked out their own specific training methods, involving programmed learning and teaching machines.

The Analysis of Behaviour, by Holland and Skinner (McGraw-Hill, New York, 1961), presents a programme for self-instruction. The reader proceeds in very small steps and cannot go on to a sentence until he has placed a missing word in a preceding sentence and understood it.

We have all been conditioned to believe something or do something at some time of our lives. Mothers are conditioning their children all the time by slapping them when they are naughty and cuddling them when they are good. Sometimes when a mother is inconsistent with her punishments and rewards, so that the child remains in a state of constant confusion, she contributes towards the development of a disturbed personality in her child. And, of course, most of us condition our children to adopt our own prejudices. Whole nations of people are conditioned to think along similar lines, and a certain amount of conditioning is necessary if we are to live together in reasonable harmony. We see evidence of conditioning when observing people of opposing ideologies. The groups have been conditioned to think differently and each group is convinced that they are right or that God is on their side. If they have been really well conditioned there can be no end to the arguments, because the conditioning has become part of the character of the people and they are incapable of seeing another point of view.

Methods of reward and punishment work reasonably well

with normal children, but how do you apply the method to autistic children, who may or may not understand the reason for the punishment, are often insensitive to pain, and don't seem to care whether you like them or not?

In experiments I have read about, the child has first been placed in some stressful situation and the situation is eased when the child co-operates. I remember reading about operant conditioning as far back as 1948 and it was not new then. I had forgotten all about it until I saw it mentioned in several books on autism and heard people discussing it in recent years. So I began reading it up again. While most of the technicalities are beyond the lay person, the articles describing the various types of experiments make very interesting reading.

When I read about operant conditioning years ago they were using rats and apes in their experiments. One rat had been trained to execute an elaborate series of responses. He was placed in a specially constructed cage and taught to tug on a string to release a marble from a container, then pick it up and stagger across the cage carrying it in his paws and drop it down a pipe two inches above the floor of the cage. I forget what his reward was, but I think he got a pellet of rat food for his trouble. It sounds like a lot of work for a pellet of rat food. He must have been a puzzled rat.

I don't know at what time autistic children replaced the rats in the experiments, but in recent years there have been dozens of papers written and many articles in various journals dealing with experiments on non-communicating children. I found one article in a journal dated 1965 which explained the teaching of some words to an autistic child through operant conditioning.

In this instance a wooden box, divided into two compartments, was used. In one the teacher sat and in the other the autistic child. The child sat in darkness. The compartments were separated by a wall with a sliding panel. This could be operated by the teacher and when she released the panel her face in the lighted compartment became visible to the child. In the child's side of the box was a little container under a dim light; into this he had to drop a ball, which then slid down a chute and into the teacher's side of the box. The teacher could release the ball for the child to pick up when she wished. When the child placed the ball in the required container a bell rang and he was rewarded by being allowed to see the teacher's face lit up for five seconds. This was only one of the rewards. Another was being given one spin in his chair, which must have revolved when the teacher pressed a button or something. He was also given sweets as a reward. Yet another reward was being allowed to hear some music.

Each time the child failed to respond within five seconds he was given five seconds in total darkness. These penalties mounted up so that if he failed twice in a row he got ten seconds' solitary.

Once the child had mastered the ball-dropping procedure he was fed his meals in a box, being given one spoonful of food or one sip of drink each time he dropped the ball in the container. After three days of this routine the child was also required to look the teacher right in the eye as well as dropping the ball in order to get each mouthful of food or drink.

In the article it was stated that for a while "difficulty was experienced" in getting the child to leave his ward each day to begin treatment because of the "change in activity involved". This sounds like the author's way of saying that the child fought savagely every inch of the way to the box.

Next the four-year-old child was taken on to extra twenty-minute sessions in the box, morning and afternoon, when he had to learn to copy simple hand movements shown him by the teacher. This was called social imitation. He found it difficult to learn to clap his hands after the teacher and spent quite a few spells in solitary over that one. After a while, though, he learned to follow simple verbal instructions and to place his hands on his face, or the teacher's face, for certain rewards.

Then began speech training. It was stated that the boy had emitted "23 random spontaneous vocalizations" on the first day of booth feeding (probably swearing in Double Holland language). He often made other "spontaneous vocalizations" over a period of time and he had been heard to make a shrill undifferentiated vowel sound on numerous occasions while in the booth. The teacher decided to use this sound to start off with. She made the sound and tried to get the child to repeat it for a reward.

When the child learned to do this the teacher proceeded to shape this sound into a word. She eventually got his vowel sounds to form the word "go" by changing the sounds slightly each time she uttered them, until she led the child to say the word "go". Every time the child got nearer the teacher's vocalization he was rewarded. Finally he learned to say the word on demand and kept it up for a few days. He then jacked up and refused to say his word. He preferred sitting in the dark to saying "go" every time the teacher requested it. After a certain period of teacher and pupil being locked in disagreement, the teacher would press her lever to release the ball back into the boy's compartment, he would pick up the ball and drop it into the container, but he wouldn't say the word. The teacher went back to saying the boy's original vowel sound, but the boy ignored her.

Finally, after a considerable time in solitary, the boy gave in and said the word again. Then the teacher, flushed with success, decided to try a second word. This had to be attempted cautiously, because as often as not in the teaching of autistic children they will only retain one word at a time. Each time a new word is learned they relinquish the old one and sometimes at the end of a lengthy speech programme they finish up with a repertoire of one word, this being retained only while the reward and punishment routine is carried out. As soon as you stop punishing them they stop talking. Not much literature is available on these children, however; people seem to prefer writing about the ones who accumulate numbers of words and retain them at least until they leave the treatment centre.

The little autistic boy in this article did learn a second word and retained his first word as well. He learned to say "my" as well as "go". The teacher gave him different rewards for the two words so as not to confuse him. After mastering his second word the little boy began to speak like a parrot, copying whatever was said to him. For instance, if his teacher asked, "How are you?" he replied, "How are you?" and if she asked him, "What is your name?" he replied, "What is your name?" If the teacher asked him, "Do you want a drink?"

he replied, "Do you want a drink?" and she wouldn't know whether he wanted a drink or not. The teacher, realizing she had reached another deadlock, decided to try and help the child make use of some of his vocabulary by employing a technique developed by Lovaas. She first taught him the sentence and the answer together: "How are you fine." Then she began to say the sentence over and over to the child, gradually fading the volume of the "How are you" part and stressing more and more the word "fine" each time. He soon learned to stop saying, "How are you", and concentrated on "fine". He paid less and less attention to the beginning of the sentence, but knew the teacher was saying it. Thus he learned to say, "Fine", every time anybody asked, "How are you?"

Then the teacher tried to get him to make use of one of his words. He was taught to say "go" each time the teacher unlocked his room to take him out.

The teacher then taught the boy to recognize the members of his family and say their names when she pointed to their photographs. After six months his parents were brought into the programme. He was allowed to return home for short periods, but not to stay overnight. Once he said "go" when he was out with his parents. After the box was no longer used to train the child the parents were occasionally allowed to watch the child being trained through a one-way vision screen. Later they were allowed to sit in the room with him while he said his words. He learned to name the members of his family when the teacher pointed to them. The parents had not been told about the teaching booth at the beginning of the programme.

After being introduced to the speech programme, the parents and brothers and sisters were given instruction by the teacher as to how they could use the child's speech at home. The whole family had to become involved in reinforcing the child's speech. If any member failed to co-operate the child could slip back. And this is where the programme could fall down. How many people are prepared to spend years, possibly the rest of their lives, in trying to keep up this endless, demanding routine of never giving the child a drink of water unless he says the right word, never giving him a mouthful of food unless he makes the right sound? With some children every meal could be dominated by this relentless routine. Some children, of course, go on to better things and learn very well without constant reinforcement, but others never get any further unless you prize every vowel out of them by punishment. The whole family has to live under the shadow of feeling guilty if they slip up in training the child.

I know families who have had their children trained in different ways, and some stick religiously to their routine, every member of the family well schooled in his instructions. But I know others who won't tolerate it. Some families couldn't possibly live under such conditions. It just depends on the personalities of the people involved. Before treatment the autistic child could be a terrible handful, a problem to every person in the family, but after treatment he could be just as tiresome in a different way. Of course, some children after a training programme become much more like normal people and seem to continue learning without the constant reinforcing, but then again other autistic children who have never had anything to do with a training programme progress quite well and learn to speak without being locked in dark boxes.

It must be realized that this one very brief, sketchy description of an experiment in operant conditioning doesn't give any idea of the whole range of possibilities that operant conditioning has opened up. People have spent many years working out and testing theories of learning. Learning machines have been devised and hundreds of books and papers have been written on many different aspects.

I read about one typewriter machine that had been tested on autistic children in the United States. The autistic children were given sessions alone with the machine. Once one key was pressed on the typewriter certain keys locked and only the keys that would make up a word could be pressed. Once a word had been spelled out it would be seen on a screen and a voice pronounced it. If a sentence were pressed out it would show up on the screen and a voice would repeat the sentence. Whole stories could be typed out and illustrated and spoken at the child's leisure. Non-speaking autistic six-year-olds had lots of fun in the story I read. They tried to copy the sounds. I think David would like a machine like that. A machine to teach autistic children seems a good idea because of their aversion to people. Many would feel more at ease with the machine and take more interest in it than they would in people at certain stages of their lives.

There is only one snag. This machine costs $30,000. But, of course, there are dozens of other methods of teaching and some of them could be helpful to autistic children.

One idea in the handling of autistic children has been developed in Brisbane by Professor Rendle-Short. It is a system for curing the autistic child's food fads. The child is placed in hospital with his mother and given three meals a day, which he can either eat or leave alone. While he is passing through some phases the autistic child becomes obsessional about certain foods and utensils. He will occasionally eat only food that is served on a certain plate or drink from a certain cup. He might scream if you try to feed him anything but hamburgers or he might cling to his bottles and fear solid foods.

I know of three parents from Victoria who took their autistic children to Brisbane for this crash feeding programme. In speaking to other mothers of autistic children about this programme, I have heard many views. Some are very much in favour of it and some very much against it. It is said to make the child more amenable to further training, almost like a form of shock treatment. The further training is carried out while he is in this state of shock.

Some people say that the inexperienced operator who conducts operant conditioning can cause severe personality damage to an autistic child, others say that the *experienced* operator who conducts operant conditioning can also cause severe personality damage to an autistic child. Then again there are others who say, "What personality?" They claim that any personality is better than the one the child already has. I think operant conditioning, used forcefully enough and without first gaining some affection from the child, could turn the child into a robot-type person. And it is not always possible to gain the affection of an autistic child. In some cases it could be easier to train him by forcing him to execute in a wooden way than to gain his affection. But, of course, some people don't mind a robot; they find the child more bearable that way.

People place importance on results today when handling autistic children. How many skills can he acquire? Never mind whether he wants to go along or not. He must keep up or be left behind. Many methods of refined punishment have been devised, such as electric shocks or letting him go hungry, in order to gain the required response.

I suppose all these methods have their place if used in moderation and with awareness that the child is a human being, not an automaton, even though he often behaves like one. Mildly afflicted children seem to respond to mild punishments, but the children who are very hard to reach are the ones that have the most to put up with. The slower the response, the longer the punishment lasts. Some children seem to me to live their entire lives in an atmosphere of nothing but punishment. Some are capable only of poor performances.

And I think it should be remembered that operant conditioning, theoretically, is considered a technical success if the pupil learns to produce a given response following presentation of a cue or stimulus in order to obtain a desired reward. He is not required to understand why. A chimpanzee has been taught to say three words, birds have been taught to repeat conversation, and rats have learned to perform complicated tasks. But do the animals know what it is all about? Is it worth anything to the animals or only to the masters? I should like to be able to believe that, in the long run, the lessons learned will make more sense to the autistic child than they did to the rats.

8

WHAT HAPPENS TO AUTISTIC CHILDREN WHEN THEY GROW UP?
How do they fit into society?

Adults who were autistic as children are hard to find. If a child had recovered from autism and was living a normal life his parents would hardly want to publicize the fact. And since in former times nobody officially diagnosed children as autistic, it would be useless to consult files on disturbed children. In any case, one would not be permitted to print confidential information from government or hospital files.

Here my many conversations with parents of disturbed and otherwise handicapped children have been most valuable. Many of these parents told me that their children, now attending normal schools, had exhibited decidedly autistic symptoms in early life, but most of them, understandably, didn't want their children to be written about. A child struggling to get by in a normal school and passing as a normal child would be handicapped if the other children knew he was recovering from an autistic state. I know one little boy who attends normal school, though obviously different from his school mates; he is withdrawn, but able to get by. When he comes home in the evenings he repeats, parrot fashion, everything the other kids have said to him during the day. No good would be done by publicizing the lives of these children.

Some parents, however, have been willing to have their

children written about, and these provide stories worth telling. It should be noted here that I have not had access to any medical records on these young people and have written the stories as told to me by the mothers. I make no claims that these people are autistic in the terms of, say, Dr Leo Kanner, who gave the first definition of autism. Since his original paper, people have been discussing other types of children with similar behaviour but unlike aetiology. I have merely described people here and called them autistic if they displayed symptoms of an autistic type at some time during their childhoods. This could be taken as a very wide view of autism.

Sammy was the first adult I met. He was a much-wanted child born nineteen years ago to middle-aged parents. His mother told me that his had been a very difficult birth, and he had been given oxygen at birth. He had been a very quiet, placid baby, who hardly ever cried. He cut teeth, sat up, and crawled like a normal child, but showed no interest in people at all and never smiled. He ignored toys, but scratched surfaces of rugs and the sides of cot and pram and spun wheels when he was about eighteen months old. He ate whatever was placed in his mouth without apparent enjoyment, never cried for food and never attempted to pick it up or hold it with his hands. Once he learned to crawl he got away from people at every opportunity, hiding behind doors, under furniture, or in cupboards. He rocked back and forth incessantly, and if he was stopped he screamed and fought savagely to get back to rocking. Though he rarely cried, he was a melancholy child, and by the time he was two years old he screamed every time he was bathed and dressed or handled in any way. He struggled violently if he was cuddled.

He spent most of his days searching for wheels he could spin and refused to be parted from several pieces of crumpled paper, which he kept squeezing in his hand. When they were wearing out his mother tried to replace them while he was asleep because once they became too small to squeeze he would thump his head on the floor or wall in anger. His mother had to employ a nurse to help bathe and dress Sammy and by the time he was three years old it took all their strength to care for him. The parents were distraught and took Sammy from one specialist to another. He was given an E.E.G. test and found to have some brain damage. As he grew older Sammy took epileptic fits.

When he was four years old Sammy's parents took him overseas to see if they could find a cure for him. They tried the United States, Germany, and England. He was given innumerable tests and at one stage one therapist tried operant conditioning.

Sammy and his mother are back in Australia now for a while, visiting relatives. His father died while they were overseas.

Sammy still doesn't speak, but understands a few commands. If his mother calls him he comes and stands beside her, waiting for her to tell him what to do next. If he is told to sit he sits. He allows his mother to dress him without putting up too much of a fight. He still ignores people, but will go for a walk with his mother if she says, "Walk", and holds his hand tightly. She has to put his coat on and get ready herself before she says, "Walk", because once she has said it he just keeps walking and won't wait. She can't stop on the way to the front door to pick up her handbag or put on her hat.

Sammy is quite gentle now and never throws tantrums, but his mother, while she is pleased that he is more manageable, is bitterly disappointed that he didn't make a better recovery. She says she has spent a fortune on Sammy and gone to the very best places with him. He can't even feed himself properly; he appears to be slightly spastic and drops things frequently.

Tablets control Sammy's epilepsy reasonably well and he is not too difficult to live with, provided he is kept to his established routine. His mother says she is thoroughly sick of having to live in the routine with Sammy, but if she gets out of it Sammy becomes bewildered and difficult. She has to do things at the same time every day. For instance, she has to take him for a walk every day at two o'clock. If it is raining she doesn't want to go, but Sammy insists on going. His mother is pleased that he is sleeping more as he gets older. He seems to be slowing down, and this suits her, she says, because she is slowing down, too. She thinks he is wearing out.

Sammy's mother has no ambition for him now and is resigned to having him as he is, but he is her only child and she has given him so much love, while he has never made the slightest sign that he cares for her. "If only Sammy would smile at me once," says his mother. But he has never smiled at anybody. Sammy is a bit like a zombie. He has learned to obey, but not to feel.

I have not met Rudy; his mother was on a visit from the United States when she told me about him. She was thirty-nine when he was born and already had one other normal child. When she was six months pregnant she had a haemorrhage and was ordered to stay in bed for the remainder of the pregnancy and given injections to prevent her miscarrying. The confinement was not difficult, but Rudy was born four weeks prematurely. He was frail at birth, but soon gained strength under the expert care of the hospital staff. His parents were thrilled to have their baby alive and well, because there had been doubts about his survival.

Rudy did a lot of crying from birth; nobody seemed to understand why. He put on weight and looked healthy, but was a most cantankerous baby. Nothing pleased him. When he was three months old his mother thought he must have been blind because he never smiled at her and didn't seem to look at anybody. The doctor did not think there was anything wrong.

At twelve months he was constantly on sedatives to calm him and at eighteen months his tantrums were so severe that his mother felt she simply could not handle him alone and asked her mother to come and live with her. Grandma didn't stay long, however, as Rudy bit and scratched her and bruised her at every opportunity. He just wanted to be left alone. He played with a mirror all the time and showed no interest in people at all. He often lay on his back on the floor and looked at the world upside-down through his mirror, becoming hysterical when interrupted for food and bathing.

Rudy's mother described him as an untamed little creature who attacked his sister if she went near him. When he wasn't looking through his mirror he played for hours spinning objects, humming tunes or rocking back and forth. Sometimes his mother tried to nurse him and rock with him, trying to gain his confidence. He fought her off vigorously and showed his irritation by banging his head on the walls and floor. Sometimes he filled in his time by banging his head on the side of the cot and at times he rattled the bars with his hands so hard that he tipped it over. He began to speak echo speech at three years and developed a phenomenal memory for words. He could repeat whole conversations heard weeks before, sing dozens of songs and recite poems, but still ignored people and bit and scratched when they tried to make friends. His mother managed to enrol him in a kindergarten when he was three and a half and he played well with the blocks and puzzles and enjoyed painting. Some of his paintings were very good, more detailed than those of other children of his age. His one overriding difficulty was his intense hatred of people. He attacked the other children constantly until they all became terrified of him and their parents had him expelled.

Brain damage showed up in an E.E.G. test when Rudy was five years old, but it was decided to try him at normal school because he was really very clever. At school he kept up with the other children and even passed some of them in reading and arithmetic, but there was always the same old trouble. He was given sedatives on and off, but his mother didn't think they helped much. He was so touchy and intolerant of other children that they only had to walk past his seat in class and throw a shadow on his work to rouse his aggression. Sometimes he attacked without any obvious reason, coming up behind some unsuspecting child. He never seriously hurt any child, mainly screaming and spitting at them. The other children all hated him and gave him a wide berth. Rudy's mother had years of complaints from other mothers and long-suffering teachers alike, but they persevered and Rudy got through primary and secondary schools. The teachers sat him apart from the rest of the class and let him work at his own pace. He was usually ahead of all the others. Maths, geography, algebra and English grammar were his best subjects, but he fell progressively behind in English expression. As he got into higher grades, although he read extremely well, he couldn't express himself or interpret what he read.

All through the years Rudy's mother kept regular appointments with therapists and psychiatrists and Rudy was always being tried on some drug or other. But his personality didn't change. His mother describes him today, at twenty-two, as a most antisocial young man who will attack anybody at any time without provocation. He is now resident in an institution for disturbed young people. His mother says she got sick of being scratched and bruised, and Rudy just got too strong for her, so she gave up. She doesn't think he will ever change. She doesn't know why he attacks. She doesn't know whether it had anything to do with the way she handled him. She just says she did the best she could and it was hard work all the way. She is past being heart-broken, though when her son first began to attack her she suffered dreadfully. She loved him and didn't want to part with him, but now she is resigned to having him live away from her. It is such a shame, she feels, to have struggled for so long with Rudy, only to have to admit defeat. Rudy almost made it; he did achieve some veneer of civilized behaviour and for a short time would calm down and appear to be maturing, but he always broke out again and lost patience with everybody. Twice he tried to kill himself. People never really meant anything to him; he just wanted to be alone. He spends most of his time alone in the hostel where he stays and talks a lot to himself. Sometimes he spends days working out arithmetical problems and loves algebra. He forms no friendships and treats the staff like furniture. He prefers a room with bars on the windows because it keeps people out.

I think the public reaction to Rudy was inevitable. You could hardly expect society to accept him. From what his mother says, I doubt if he will ever learn to live with people.

Georgie is a tired-looking boy who prefers to be left alone. He likes watching television and if spoken to while the television is switched on does not answer. His mother has to prod him into any form of activity, but once prodded he can perform simple tasks. He can bathe and dress himself, help prepare meals, help with the garden, shop, tidy his room, and make his bed, but does not like any form of physical activity. He prefers sitting on the beach to swimming and if he goes for a walk with the family usually makes for the first park bench.

Georgie's mother says she had a normal pregnancy and confinement, but suspects she had a mild form of hepatitis during the pregnancy. Georgie was an aloof baby from the start; his mother thought he had a "far-away look in his eyes". He passed through stages of screaming, laughing, and doing nothing during his babyhood, and could switch from one mood to the other in a matter of seconds. He often ignored his mother completely when she tried to feed him and stayed awake for long periods at a time. He clung to his bottles till he was four years old and then suddenly weaned himself in one day and began to eat normally. Sometimes he ate so much that he made himself vomit, but appeared not to care. Doctors were never able to find anything physically wrong with him. He was given blood tests, urine tests, and an E.E.G. test.

Georgie saved cardboard boxes and at one stage had his room full of them. He preferred square ones to oblong ones. If anyone moved his boxes to clean the room he flew into violent rages and banged his head against the wall.

At the age of eighteen months Georgie spoke his first very clear words and everyone thought he was very intelligent because he could copy anything anyone said. He repeated words after hearing them once, but he never made any attempt to use them or to make conversation. He could also hum tunes. He avoided the word "I". He never asked for anything; he just screamed and banged his head on the floor till his mother discovered what he wanted. He appeared insensitive to heat and cold and appeared not to feel pain. He didn't appear to like his mother and father and behaved as though they weren't there.

When his speech improved his mother tried him at kindergarten. He got on quite well while everyone left him alone. When the children played singing and marching games he watched out of the corner of his eye, but made no move to join them. If the teacher tried to carry him round with the children he kicked and bit her, so they left him till he was ready and after a year he began to march and hum the tunes apart from the other children. He enjoyed sticking his fingers into lumps of Plasticine and sometimes tried to eat it, but

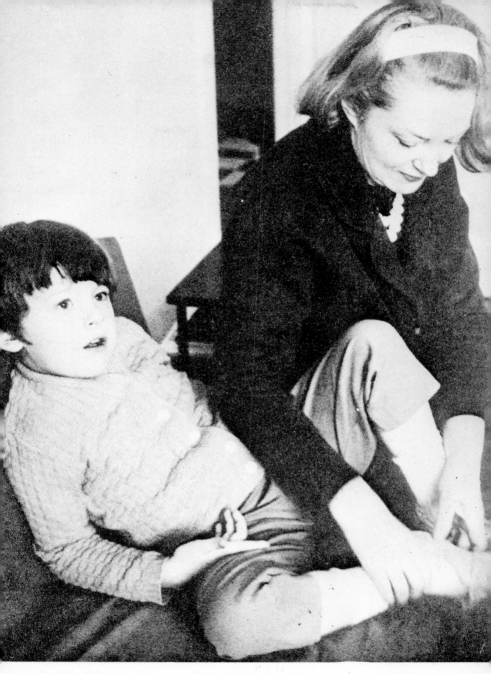

David in a typical "getting dressed" pose. When you try to dress him (having first caught him) he turns himself into a rag doll and his limbs flop all over the place, so that you have to hold the limb in position as well as try to get the garment on.

Almost a family portrait. Ellen and I tried to encourage David to smile, but he didn't quite make it on demand. This was just after his sixth birthday.

didn't model anything. He took up painting squares.

He always carried two little hand-mirrors with him and placed them down carefully when he was otherwise engaged, but there was a terrible scene if one of the other children tried to look at his mirrors. Once when a friendly little girl placed a third mirror alongside his two, Georgie became hysterical and threw his mirrors at the wall and trod on both of them. He was heart-broken for days after this and it took about a week for him to settle. Not long after he stole another mirror from his mother's handbag and then found another mirror in a visitor's handbag. Then he settled down again to keeping the two mirrors with him all the time.

He was accepted at a private school for normal children at the age of seven (that's when he was finally toilet trained) and managed to keep up with the lessons. He could write very well and spell perfectly, but he still failed to make full use of the words he had mastered and could never write a composition. He could manage arithmetic and loved music and painting, though he only painted squares. He always had a good sense of rhythm, and when he was eight his parents bought him a set of drums, on which he beat out exotic rhythms at all hours of the day and night. Sometimes he refused to eat for days on end and became pale and listless, and some days he just slept. Then he would start eating again and his health and appetite would be normal for a time.

Sometimes Georgie was violent towards his two sisters, both older than himself, and would lock himself in his room and sob and scream for hours. Nobody ever knew why. He seemed happier when his sisters went to boarding-school. At school Georgie's tantrums were so bad that the teachers occasionally sent him home, but on the whole they were amazingly tolerant, and Georgie's mother is full of praise for the years of patient work they put in with him. They treated him the same as all the others in class and tried to make him keep up.

After the age of twelve Georgie's tantrums eased off altogether and he made a big leap forward in his understanding of how to behave himself. He seemed to mature, and now at the age of seventeen he appears calm—too calm. His mother thinks he has just burned himself out and is too weary to throw any more tantrums. He has learned to accept people

H

and tries to make polite conversation, but is only at home with certain subjects. He likes to talk about moon travel and can remember all the names of planets and astronauts and dates of moon flights. He knows the distances between various planets and can estimate how long it would take to travel from one planet to another at such and such a speed. But after talking to him for a while you realize that he just doesn't understand the concept of space. He only understands travel along the surface of the earth. Even if he sees a planet in the sky, he believes you go along the earth's surface to get to it. He can't imagine leaving the earth.

Georgie left school at the age of sixteen, after completing nine years of normal schooling. But the last two years he had not been able to pass exams, even with extra tuition. His brain seemed to be tiring and he could not keep up. He is now easy to live with and, though he still prefers to spend a lot of time alone, when he does join the members of his family he is very pleasant and they are all very fond of him.

He has no sense of humour and no understanding of anything abstract. When his sisters laugh at a funny incident he asks them to explain it to him, but he never gets the point and remains solemn and unsmiling as a Sardinian widow through the telling of all humorous anecdotes.

Georgie dismissed his painting teacher because she tried to persuade him to paint something other than squares. He still takes music lessons, but his teacher knows better than to comment on Georgie's piano playing, or he might follow the art teacher. His parents think Georgie should continue to take music lessons, even though he is not improving. He enjoys having the teacher sit still while he plays to him. It fills in his time.

For many years Georgie paid regular visits to a psychiatrist, but now only goes occasionally, when the family returns to England. His mother says that the psychiatrist helped him gain confidence. He let Georgie talk about himself and paint squares on the walls. It was very expensive but well worth it.

In talking to Georgie's mother, I gather that she has always been very patient with him and allowed him a good deal of freedom. She says she never slapped him during his hysterical outbursts. She has spared no effort or expense to give her son a pleasant life, and gave him added protection when she felt he needed it. When he was twelve Georgie showed signs of wanting to have his mother around and began to fear being left alone at night. His mother sat up all night with him sometimes. He wouldn't have her in the room with him, but wanted her to sit in the doorway where he could keep her in sight.

Georgie developed unevenly. Although he kept up with school lessons reasonably well, he kept chewing and sucking objects like a young baby. If there was a new piece of furniture in the house Georgie wanted to feel it with his hands and his eyes closed. He used to rub new curtains against his cheek and roll on the floor whenever he saw a new carpet. His mother didn't object to any of this.

Georgie has always disliked dogs and horses and hates to see members of his family ride.

Georgie's mother phoned me when she heard that I was writing a book about my son David. She thought readers might be interested to hear about a boy who had grown out of his autistic symptoms.

I shook hands with Georgie at the front door and he and his mother came inside. I poured them a cool drink of apricot and passionfruit juice, which Georgie said tasted very nice. Then he wanted to know where I got the passionfruit and apricots. I explained that I had bought the mixture in a tin. He asked me which shop. When I told him he asked his mother if they could drive past this shop on the way home and buy some of the juice. She agreed. Georgie then wanted to know where the fruit had been grown. I had no idea. He asked if he could look at the tin. I took him out to the kitchen and he read every word on the label with the greatest interest, then asked if he could keep the label. When we returned to the lounge his mother tried to change the subject, mentioning the nice garden across the street. Georgie ignored her.

He looked at me intently for a minute then asked politely, "Do your legs go all the way up?"

Georgie had only recently become aware of human anatomy and had begun to ask all kinds of odd questions about the shape of people. His mother confided to me that she was steeling herself for the "why does Auntie Mavis have bumps?" type of question in public.

Later that day Georgie said to me, "You have long arms today." I was wearing a sleeveless blouse.

"What about your mother's arms? Aren't they long?" I asked.

"No," he answered, "they are very short." She was wearing three-quarter-length sleeves. Georgie thinks your limbs begin where your clothes end.

Georgie's mother told me that he was often confused about which people were men and which were women. I wondered how he did tell them apart, and asked him what might appear to be a silly question, but Georgie thought it was reasonable.

"Is your mother a man or a woman?"

"A woman," he replied.

"How do you know?"

"She is wearing a dress," he said.

I was wearing slacks. "What about me, am I a man or a woman?" I asked.

"You are a woman," he said.

"How do you know?"

"You have long hair."

I wanted to get some more answers from Georgie. I found a coloured picture magazine with a picture of a hippie with long hair, slacks, a loose-fitting jacket, a necklace and a beard.

"Is that a man or a woman?" I asked.

"That's a man," answered Georgie.

"How do you know?"

"He has a beard," said Georgie.

I pointed to a picture of another hippie dressed similarly with long hair but no beard.

"Is that a man or a woman?" I asked.

Georgie looked confused and didn't answer. I could hardly blame him.

Later, when the bewildered look had left Georgie's face, I asked him, "Georgie, are you a man or a woman?"

"I am a man," he replied.

I then showed him the picture of the hippie with the beard again.

"This is a man with a beard," I said. "Do you have a beard?"

Georgie didn't answer. I then showed him his face in a hand-mirror, and asked again, "Do you have a beard?"

"I don't have a beard," said Georgie.

"Why don't you have a beard?" I asked.

"I don't havě a beard," he repeated, without answering my question.

"Georgie," I said, "do you shave every day?"

"I shave every morning at seven thirty," said Georgie.

"What would happen if you didn't shave?"

"My father would tell me to shave."

"But what would happen if your father didn't tell you to shave?" I wanted to know.

Georgie hesitated, he seemed to be putting two and two together. Finally he spoke.

"My mother would tell me to shave," he said simply.

Georgie is quite innocent about sex at present. His father and mother have tried to explain it to him, but he just doesn't understand. His curiosity about human shapes is growing, however, and his questions could land him in a lot of trouble if asked in public. They would sound wonderfully cute from a three-year-old, but it is quite different for a young man of seventeen. His mother doesn't want to deprive him of the necessary experience of going out alone to shop and mix with people, but she is very concerned about him all the time he is out of her sight.

Georgie attends a church discussion group and so far there have been no complaints about him, but his mother dreads the day when he might ask some embarrassing questions.

His compliments are probably worse than his questions. He has stored up a lot of sentences, nice things for saying when you first meet people, but he gets the compliments for women mixed up with the compliments for men. He recently ruined the dignity of one of his mother's "at homes" by asking a lady guest if she was a man or a woman and complimenting a man guest on his hair-style. It wouldn't have been so bad if the man hadn't been bald.

Although there is no financial need for Georgie to work, he could probably hold down some sort of job if it were not for his habit of falling asleep in the middle of the day. And he is sleeping more as he gets older. Sometimes he falls asleep in the middle of his evening meal and his sisters call him Georgie the Doormouse.

Georgie's mother doesn't mind how much he sleeps. She says he might just as well be asleep as doing anything else and at least she knows he is out of mischief.

9

IN SPITE OF DANNY'S NORMAL APPEARANCE, AT OUR FIRST meeting I could tell he was one of "them"—one of the aloof ones. I have seen the look so often. He was shy when I first spoke to him and didn't look at my face. Carol, his mother, brought him over to meet me after reading about my son David in the *Herald*. She told me that David resembled Danny in many ways when Danny was small. Many incidents came back to her as she read about the problems I had with David.

Danny was one of the most successful young adults with a history of autism whom I had met. His mother gave me permission to print his story and she kept in touch with me over a period of twelve months, telling me everything that happened. This was most interesting, since I wanted to know about society's reaction to a former autistic child.

Danny was sufficiently advanced to go out alone. He could shop alone, understood the value of money, could travel on trains, could speak well, and appeared quite normal. He rode his bike all over the neighbourhood and went swimming alone. He could take care of his needs at home, make his bed, dress himself, and if necessary prepare a meal. Carol has a never-ending stream of funny stories to tell and takes all her troubles good-naturedly.

Danny was Carol's first child. He is now eighteen years old.

When she first conceived Carol was ill for a few months and then miscarried. She was very depressed, but decided that when she recovered sufficiently she would try for another child. But about eight months after her original conception Danny was born. She doesn't know quite how it happened, but thinks that she must have been carrying twins and miscarried only one. There are twins in the family.

The baby was delivered by Caesarean section prematurely, and both Carol and her husband were delighted that all had gone well. The baby appeared quite healthy, but had a harelip and had to undergo an operation in the first twelve months and another at three years.

Carol had to spoon-feed Danny for a long time when he was tiny because he had difficulty in sucking, but he soon put on weight. Nevertheless, Carol noticed something odd about him from birth that she couldn't explain. She says he had a "sad empty look behind the eyes as though there was nothing there", and he still has it.

He was about two and a half before other people began to notice anything unusual about him. For instance, he played only with mirrors and looked at everything upside-down. Carol's relatives used to say, "Don't let him do that, people will think he's queer." But Danny continued to play with mirrors and ignored toys completely. He struggled against any change, wagged pencils back and forth, and flicked things in front of his eyes as though hypnotized. He was fascinated by spinning tops.

When he was three Danny underwent his second operation on his lip. He had to stay in hospital for three weeks and Carol was advised not to visit him for fear of upsetting him. When she finally did go to the hospital to pick him up she noticed a hurt look in his eyes and he was stranger than ever.

But he seemed quite intelligent and could pick out all the letters of the alphabet at three and could read beautifully at five, though he didn't seem to understand what he read. At four years he spoke very clearly, but it was mostly echo speech; he just copied conversations. It was very difficult to get through to him and he didn't seem to understand what was required of him, but Carol managed to find a very understanding kindergarten teacher who persevered with him until he was able to attend regular school with normal children. One thing in Danny's favour was that he was never violent. He sometimes made funny noises and did little dances, but never flew into rages the way some autistic children do. He was lost if some change took place; he had to do things exactly the same way each day.

Danny learned to write and became good at spelling. He coped well with arithmetic, algebra, English grammar and parsing, but was all at sea in English expression. He couldn't improvise or make anything up.

They bought Danny a bike, but had to teach him to ride by holding him on the seat, placing his feet on the pedals and pushing them by hand. When Danny finally got the hang of it he just kept riding in a straight line, crashing into walls and fences. But eventually he did learn to turn corners and was very pleased with himself.

Carol considers Danny's years at technical school as his most progressive. There he developed an awareness of himself to the extent of wanting to join in with the group. And the teachers tried to help all the way. Carol has nothing but praise for the Victorian Education Department. She says that Danny gave them a puzzling time, but they kept trying to keep his work level with that of the other children and did what they could to help him socially.

For the most part the children accepted him and occasionally one tried to encourage him to get his homework done, but sometimes they used him for a bit a fun. They knew he would do anything they told him without understanding what the consequences would be. Once they told him to tell a teacher she was a pregnant bitch, and poor Danny did just as he was told. Carol was often summoned to explain things and smooth things over with the staff. Another of the boys' pranks was telling Danny to chase girls, so Danny chased them. The girls' mothers were always complaining. Carol tried to explain that Danny didn't understand, but she had a hard job.

Danny has no idea of what is expected of him socially and makes blunders constantly. He tries to copy other people, but says the wrong things at the wrong times.

Carol and her husband have tried to explain the facts of

life to Danny, but he just looks blank and says he already knows the difference between men and women. Men wear men's clothes and women wear women's clothes. Danny can't grasp anything abstract. He has to see something before he understands it. The human reproductive system remains a mystery to him.

When he was seventeen Danny had to leave school. The teachers had gone as far as they could with him. He could read, but understood little of what he read, and he was simply incapable of carrying out an assignment. He still could not write a composition, his concentration was poor and he stopped after every few lines. He had an immature outlook to feature design and colour. A lot of the time he was quiet and withdrawn, but sometimes he bombarded teachers with questions. Occasionally he waved his arms in the air and danced on tiptoe with a look of trance-like ecstasy on his face.

Danny's memory was fantastic and he could remember long lists of words, dates, and conversations heard years before. He could resume a conversation in exactly the right place when revisiting friends after a long period of time. He was rather like a computer and had to be programmed constantly, but he could not process much of the information he had stored up.

Carol is grateful to the teachers for keeping Danny at school as long as they did. He was not able to pass exams, but normal school has certainly helped him. He still has little ability to understand people, but what he knows of social behaviour he learned through being with normal children. Not all he learned has been good, but the experience was essential.

Carol takes Danny out as much as possible and helps him to mix with people at every opportunity now that he has left school. She has other younger children and is very busy, but tries to keep him aware socially by explaining what you do and don't do when talking to people. She has had him taught typing and supervises his practice every day, and he has joined a boys' club. He types quite well, but needs some help occasionally if something new crops up. He has trouble folding paper to fit into different-sized envelopes.

Danny answers the phone, but his voice is flat. He used to forget what people told him over the phone, but now he remembers and gives messages to the right people. He is learning all the time, but Carol can't let up. If she does he slips back.

Sometimes Carol worries while Danny is out alone on his bike. She never knows whom he might meet or what he might say, but she realizes she has to let him develop and learn and gain confidence in himself. And he is proud of going out alone. His mother tells him he mustn't dance while out in the street, but he is likely to forget, particularly on windy days. He becomes exhilarated in the wind and throws back his head, throws out his arms, and twirls round and round, smiling up at the sky. Sometimes Carol sees him dancing in her front garden and calls out, "I can see you", and he stops. But he often sneaks in a few twirls if he thinks she is not around. Carol hates having to stop him from dancing because it is something he enjoys and does spontaneously, but what can she do? How will people regard a grown man who looks normal and suddenly starts to dance in the street?

One day while Carol and Danny were visiting me Danny was sitting in a chair looking out of the window while Carol and I were chatting. Suddenly, out of the blue, Danny began to smile, a deep, beautiful smile that spread over his whole face. Even his eyes were smiling. Carol, hoping to draw him into the conversation, asked, "Why are you smiling, Danny?"

"I don't know," he answered, "but sometimes when I am by myself and the sun is shining it just comes on my face and my mouth goes like this." And he pushed his mouth up at the corners to show us.

There is an air of gentleness about Danny, but he gives the impression of being quite remote, as though he is living separately from the rest of us, just looking in on the world. He doesn't laugh at the things other people laugh at, but he goes into paroxysms of mirth at the sight of anything upside-down. And for days after seeing anything flash on the television screen upside-down he keeps on chuckling every time he thinks of it. Sometimes he just calls out, "Upside-down!" and bursts out laughing.

Once Carol took the whole family to see the film *Oliver Twist*. Danny sat quietly till Oliver took his bowl up to ask for more. As soon as Oliver said, "More", Danny burst into loud laughter. They quietened him down, but every so often he broke out into chuckles. This is still one of his jokes, and now and then he says to himself, "More", and rocks with mirth. As Carol says, it's not easy to understand the way Danny's mind works.

Danny was very interested in the moon landing and watched the whole thing on television. He told his mother, "The moon came down to the earth and some men got on it." When she tried to explain that the men went to the moon he simply didn't understand. As far as he was concerned the moon came to the earth.

I have often seem examples of autistic children developing unevenly. Danny is an uneven developer. This is clearly demonstrated in his favourite television programmes. He likes "It's Academic", a programme where high-school students answer questions—and he knows most of the answers —and "Fred Bear", a children's programme with a man dressed up as a bear.

When a close relative died some time ago Carol was worried about what effect it might have on Danny. But when she told him he just looked at her calmly as though she had said the person had gone on a holiday. He didn't seem to mind. I don't think he understands death.

There has been an enormous change in Danny over the last seven years. His confidence has increased considerably, but he still fears change. He still can't improvise. Any deviation in his routine causes him anxiety. He gets up at the same time every morning, ten to seven, and likes to know exactly what is going to happen. When his mother tries to accustom him to variation from time to time he says anxiously, "Things aren't always the same, are they?"

If he gets on one subject he likes to stay on it. He is likely to carry a conversation about weather to a discussion on all aspects of temperatures. His mother can handle this trait and eases him on to other subjects, but it is tiresome for strangers. If someone wrote him a note asking him to do something he would be likely to concentrate on correcting the spelling instead of carrying out the instructions. He likes to put things right.

Sometimes Carol does the things Danny does to demonstrate for him just what it looks like to other people. For instance, she shows him what he looks like when he does his funny little dances and he laughs.

Danny loves the story of Mary Poppins and reads it over and over. He enjoyed the film, too, especially the part where Mary floats down the bannister and flies in the air. He never tires of it.

One of Carol's biggest problems is that when Danny meets other teenage lads they tease him mercilessly. He tries to join in with them, but finishes up losing his temper and swearing at them. This was one bad thing he learned at secondary school. Carol is afraid he might get into a fight, and she knows he will get the blame if anybody gets hurt. He is the one that is supposed to be odd. Danny really goes to pieces when the boys call him funny names. They say things like, "Hullo, Buffalo Bill, here comes Buffalo Bill from the U.S.A." Danny calls back, "No, my name is Danny and I come from England", then they come back with, "No, you're not, you're an Eskimo and you come from the North Pole." "No!" shouts Danny. "My name is Danny and I come from England."

Carol tries to explain to Danny when he comes home that the boys are only teasing. But Danny doesn't understand other people's jokes; he only understands his own, and he takes everything so seriously.

Several parents of autistic children have told me that their children can't take a joke, and they especially hate to be called by another name. I wonder whether this has anything to do with feeling uncertain about identity. At what age does a child become confident about his own identity? As an experiment, I tried to joke with a few normal three-year-olds and called them different names. "Hullo, Buffalo Bill," I said to one little boy. He argued seriously with me and assured me that his name was Robin. Another little boy became quite cross when I called him Buffalo Bill and threatened to shoot me down. When I called a little girl Buffalo Bill she seemed less worried than the boys, but told me I was wrong in very firm tones.

They didn't think it was a joke, even though I was smiling when I said it and tried to joke with them. They didn't like being kidded about their names. On the other hand, when I said, "Let's play a game of cowboys and Indians, and you be Buffalo Bill and you be Indians", they were happy to oblige. They didn't mind being someone else when I told them it was to be a game.

With five-year-olds the reaction was similar, but not as intense. They were half inclined to join in with the joke, but were not completely sure of themselves.

I tried out the experiment on only one eight-year-old. A little boy called in to play draughts with Ellen one afternoon after school. "Hullo, Buffalo Bill," I called out, smiling. He looked surprised then raised one eyebrow and looked superior.

Later I heard him laughing as he told Ellen, "I think your mother's lost some of her marbles. She thinks my name's Buffalo Bill."

"Is she still on about that?" said Ellen. "She's just experimenting for that book she's writing."

"Sounds like a mad book," said her partner and went on with the game of draughts.

After leaving school, Danny was at a loss. He used to ride his bike up to the school gate and watch the pupils enter and leave the grounds. Sometimes he tried to talk to the teachers.

Carol tried to help him keep busy each day; he typed and went swimming. It had been suggested to Carol that he should go on the waiting list for enrolment at a Commonwealth rehabilitation centre in order to help him prepare for a job. Carol didn't think they would ever have encountered anyone quite like Danny before, but it seemed worth a try. This centre catered for many different types of handicaps and had a very good reputation. Danny would board there; the idea was to help him become more independent and to find out what type of employment he could fit into and train him. Danny waited for a year before he was admitted, and in the meantime Carol tried to get him to mix with people and take in as much experience as possible.

One day when Danny and Carol came to my place I asked Danny if he would like to make up something on the typewriter while I prepared lunch. I knew he could copy very well, but I wanted to see how much he could make up. He stuck to facts. He typed these neat sentences:

Today is Wednesday, 11th of June.
I will be eighteen on the 14th June.
That will be in three days time.
This morning I got up at ten minutes to seven.
The time is now one o'clock.
People usually have lunch about this time.
We arrived here about quarter to eleven.
Half the year has nearly gone.
There is a dog in the back garden here.
We went to England on the 22nd December, 1967.
Sometimes I watch my children come out of school.
It is a lovely day today with the sun shining.
At home I type invoices.
Invoices are hard sometimes.
June 21st is the longest day of the year in England.
June 22nd is the longest day of the year in England.
December 21st is the shortest day of the year in England.
December 22nd is the shortest day of the year in England.

While Danny was waiting to be admitted to the rehabilitation centre Carol had two anonymous phone calls from mothers in the area asking her not to let Danny out because he made them nervous. Danny would sometimes stand in front of former school friends' houses and watch for the children to come out and go to school. Occasionally he tried to speak to them, but mostly he just stood and watched. One day one of the fathers came out and asked Danny what he was doing, standing in front of his house. Danny just said, "Nothing." "Well, move on," said the father, "or I'll call the police to have you moved."

Carol tries to prepare Danny for other people's reactions to him, but he really has to undergo an experience before he can understand it. Even then he often remains puzzled. One day his mother told him to change his clothes hurriedly as they were going out unexpectedly. He stripped off naked in his room with the door open while a visitor stood in the hall, and had no idea what all the fuss was about.

I was worried when Carol phoned me one day to say that she had to go into hospital for a few weeks. I said I would phone Danny from time to time, though Carol said Danny didn't seem to care when she said she was leaving him for a while. Danny's father and other members of the family were well able to help him get by and Carol knew she would be able to phone from the hospital.

When I phoned him Danny did not seem to be at all worried about being left alone through the day. He spent a great deal of his time watching television serials. The only things he seemed to worry about were the people in the serials, and if somebody was missing for one episode he always mentioned it to me. Every time I phoned I said, "Hullo, Danny, this is Joan Hundley speaking", and he answered, "Hullo, Joan Hundley." When I asked after his mother he always answered that she was "very well, thank you", without appearing to give it much thought.

Strangely enough, Danny's voice lost some of its flatness while his mother was in hospital. He began to copy her inflections. Carol has a very expressive voice and this seemed to register with Danny for the first time. I think this must have been the result of speaking to her on the phone so much.

When Carol arrived home from hospital Danny met her at the door and said, "Mum, it's good to have you back." Carol said that was the nicest thing he had ever said to her.

Danny had got used to the idea that he would some day be going to live for a while in the rehabilitation centre and seemed content to do so. He was anxious to learn all he could to help him get a job. But when word finally came that they were ready for him he became upset and, for the first time in his life, his mother saw him cry.

"I don't want to leave home," he said. This in itself meant that Danny was improving.

Danny seemed to settle in the centre at first and really tried to do his best, but unfortunately he had little interest in the handwork taught there and after a while he began to copy the physical disabilities of his fellow pupils. Carol said that when he came home on week-ends he walked stiff-legged and began to slow down, moving like a robot. He also became depressed. They drugged him heavily, but Carol thought this made him worse. When he came home one week-end he was supposed to take seven tranquillizers a day. He appeared to be in a state of complete confusion and began to vomit. Finally it was decided that this centre was just not suitable for Danny. So Danny came home and soon regained his composure and confidence.

The big problem still stands. How can Danny get a job? Who wants to employ such a boy? He is very anxious to contribute. He wants to be a part of things, to have the opportunity of using what talents he has developed. It is not a question of money. His parents can manage financially, but Danny wants to feel necessary. He has developed that far.

Carol arranged to see a psychiatrist and therapist with the Mental Health Authority and I am sure they will do all they can to help. They will have met other people resembling Danny, and they will be able to gain his confidence and perhaps even lead him on to fresh accomplishments. I have no doubt that Danny will fit in quite well with the institution atmosphere and the regular activities there. I don't think he will cause them a moment's anxiety. But is that what Danny really needs? Will a spell with the Mental Health Authority do any good for Danny when he comes home again and tries to shop at the corner store? Will the people he meets understand him any better? I think that, in the long run, Danny's success or failure will depend on the man and woman in the street.

I see Danny as a strange adult, intelligent in some ways, but very naive, incapable of manipulating his environment, believing everything he sees, doing everything he is told. A complete innocent.

Danny is different things to different people.

To the doctor who performed the delicate operation that delivered him when he was born he was a complete success.

To the doctors who operated on his harelip he was a com plete success.

To the teacher who nursed him through kindergarten years he was an unusual little boy who took a lot of understanding, but very interesting, and she still takes the trouble to write to him from England.

To the teachers who pushed him through primary school, he was a challenge and well worth the struggle, because they thought he would get there if they could just get through to him.

I

To some of them he was an embarrassment. They never knew what he was going to say. And people can't believe that he is entirely innocent. How could they? They have never heard of anyone like him before.

To the boys who mixed with him at school he didn't seem a bad sort of kid, a bit quiet, but they liked him well enough and tried to include him in some activities, though he seemed a bit stupid at times. And his mental awkwardness made him stand out, so they thought he was funny sometimes. And it was fun having someone who always did what you told him to do.

To the psychiatrists and therapists who have seen Danny from time to time over the years he is a pleasure. They always congratulate his mother and tell her how well he is coming on. And Danny makes a very good impression. He tries to co-operate.

To his mother and father, who love him, he is a constant cause of anxiety. They feel for him and his hurts are their hurts. They live with his awkwardness twenty-four hours a day.

To society Danny is a nothing, because so far society doesn't know Danny exists.

And what about the law? It is possible that Danny could fall foul of the law and not have any idea of what he had done wrong. How would he stand up to being charged with an offence? I don't think innocence is much of a defence. And who would believe him? If he were forced to fend for himself alone outside an institution, without his family to guide and advise and protect him, I see no reason why he shouldn't join the ranks of vagrants who shuffle in and out of jail year after year, serving short sentences for minor offences. Vagrants form a large proportion of our prison admissions. They are people who can't cope with their environment, the ones who have not been tailored to fit in and who make society look untidy. Danny could easily join the homeless ones, those unable to stay married, the socially mal-adjusted, the ex-mental hospital patients, the grown-up institution children, some suffering from dyslexia, the alcoholics, the lost people of society. One of the quickest ways of going to jail in our society is to do nothing. If you have nowhere to sleep, nothing in your pocket, and can't keep a job you can easily spend your life in and out of jail.

There are many ways that Danny could get into trouble. He is developing a liking for being with people, but his taste in literature is on a par with that of a young child. What if he were to seek out a child of his own literary mental age to talk about books and television programmes? How would the public react to a man who does funny little dances taking small children aside to talk?

I remember when my husband was supervising an evening club for retarded boys one of the lads (a man of thirty-three) came in bruised and bleeding. He had stopped in the street to share his sandwiches with a little girl, and two men had beaten him and told him not to talk to little girls or they would call the police next time. This man had the mental age of a child of eight and had little idea of sex. Some people seem to think that behind every tattered brain there lurks a sex fiend. But you can't blame the public for being worried. Most people don't know the difference between one handicapped person and another. If one mentally deranged person commits a crime every mentally handicapped person becomes suspect, and the innocent ones don't have a voice.

Many handicapped people I have met have no idea of sex. Giving sex instruction to mentally handicapped children is a headache; this is just one more problem for parents of autistic children. Most parents I meet don't know how to steer their normal children through the intricacies of sex avoidance during the teens, let alone their handicapped ones. And in our society there is nothing respectable for any teenager, handicapped or otherwise, to do with a sex urge.

And so Danny goes his innocent way, trying to follow the teenagers around on his bike and wanting to be like them. Recently he began following their lead when they spent time in newsagents' shops reading comics and magazines and browsing through the new books. Danny keeps to his own taste in literature on these jaunts, looking for books about Hansel and Gretel, his current favourite story.

Danny has no idea that he is a suspected problem to some members of the public and is quite confident that he will get a job like everyone else. I think part of his confidence is due to the fact that his parents have such faith in him. After all their years of steering him through difficult and embarrassing situations and watching his progress with such pride, it seems unbelievable that he should almost make it, but not quite. Carol is very realistic, however, and knows what she is up against. At the time of writing Danny is still full of hope for the future. Danny thinks he is ready for society. But I wonder if society is ready for Danny.

In deciding whether or not to have the autistic-type adult moving out in society, we should have to ask ourselves only one question: Will he harm anybody? If his family wants to keep him at home, or even if he has no family, will society put up with his eccentric behaviour? I think it will if it knows he does no harm. Many such adults are very gentle. But society is frightened of anyone who doesn't quite fit in. At no time before in the history of man have we had so many personal restrictions placed on us, and we are giving up small portions of our freedom every year. We tolerate this in order to gain the advantages of living together in large technological societies. But there are plenty of rules that are not strictly necessary, many old laws that we don't need any more. We find ourselves bending to new laws as well as to old ones that have been made obsolete by the advances in medicine and technology. Legally and socially we have not yet caught up with the age we live in. As we continue to reduce the infant mortality rate we shall have to face the fact that we could be changing the character of human beings. We could be producing more people who have difficulty in conforming, more who are dependent but eccentric, unable to grasp the true nature of their complicated environment.

At present we recognize three official categories of people who can't be left out in society; physically ill, mentally ill, and criminals. A person who does not fit in and is not obviously sick tends to be included with criminals.

The socially disoriented person who breaks the law through innocence, but does society no harm, does not belong anywhere. At present we only have prison for incompetent lawbreakers. And incompetent people do seem to break the law often. I think many prisoners could live in the community with some form of accommodation provided without prison security measures. It is unhealthy to isolate people from their own society. To imprison the socially disoriented person only makes him more disoriented. Many vagrants now go to prison because there is no other accommodation for them. And I think we have to let go the idea that all odd people who don't fit in can be cured. I think we should loosen our social structure a little to include them, so that the things they do through ignorance or innocence are tolerated by society.

One problem, of course, is the fact that people administering the law can't visualize an institution without some form of punishment. An institution for socially awkward people where they could come and go like other people in the community is not yet part of our national thinking, in spite of the lead given by our Mental Health Authorities. Odd people should be allowed to go for walks in the parks or attend concerts, to buy their own tobacco and soap and select their own clothes in shops like everyone else. Some of these people should be on pensions, others could do part-time jobs, and some might be capable of full-time employment. If possible they should all be required to pay small sums for board.

I know that some Churches have hostel-type accommodation and provide meals for homeless people, but this should be a national thing. These incompetent people should have official recognition.

10

DAVID'S INTERESTS CONTINUE TO SPREAD. HE HAS BECOME interested in knitting-wool. He will toss a ball of it around, holding one strand twisted round a finger, till the ball becomes completely unravelled. When it is loose and matted, Ellen says he has knitted a wig. Once he could not even touch wool because of his delicate skin; now he plays with it for hours and it doesn't harm him. He loves to get to Ellen's knitting and unravel it. She has been knitting a scarf for nearly a year now, and doesn't look like finishing it. Whenever I find David unravelling it I take it away and pick up the stitches, but he has more time for unravelling than she and I have for knitting.

He is also interested in hair-ribbons, lengths of string, shoe-laces. He flicks these up and down with a sort of whip-cracking technique which eventually makes a string of knots in them. If he works on a belt for a few hours it becomes knotted right up to where he is holding it.

He is still incapable of dressing himself, but one day recently I saw him trying to put on a pair of pants. He had chosen a new pair of Ellen's lace-trimmed briefs. They were a sort of lime-green colour with wavy yellow lines all over, and he was very taken with them. Sitting on the ground, he put his two feet through one leg and pulled the pants up as far as his knees, upside-down. Although hobbled and barely able to walk, he was very proud of having donned a garment and would not take them off. He tottered round the house for an hour or more, falling over from time to time. This was his first attempt to adorn himself.

David is now learning to recognize a few words he hears on television. There is an advertisement for a certain shampoo that evokes a definite response from him. At the sight of a lady lathering masses of froth into her hair, he makes for the door and when the singing starts, "Wash your hair, shiny and healthy . . .", he holds his hands protectively over his head and runs outside as fast as his legs will carry him. Once I heard him utter, "No no", as he ran.

Ellen told me one day that the people of Double Holland were so proud of little David's progress that they had decided to hold a splendid ceremony and crown him their king.

The coronation was held one Saturday morning. It was a splendid turn-out with King Audie wearing a paper crown encrusted with jewels painted on with watercolours. Ellen had spent a whole afternoon making it, and half-way through the ceremony King Audie began to eat it. But the people of Double Holland didn't mind; they laughed and laughed and had a wonderful time. Mr and Mrs Slubar attended to the catering. There was fruit juice, and bread-and-butter sprinkled with hundreds and thousands, and chocolate-flavoured ice-cream, and some toffee apples. The feast lasted twenty-four hours. I didn't attend myself because I was tied up with the washing, but Ellen kept me posted. Little Billy joined in, too, and looked after the twelve white horses that drew the golden royal coach through the streets of Double Holland while the people cheered and cheered. From time to time, because the procession was too slow, King Audie left the decorated kitchen chair which doubled as the royal coach, but the people didn't mind; they thought it was great fun when their king walked round among them, hopping on one leg and calling out, "Oi oi!" or "Hy yi yi!"

Ellen told me later that Prime Minister Hon Sting thought the ceremony was such a success that he was going to arrange ten coronations a year, just to make the people happy. That's the way things are in Double Holland. They all love a good celebration and they dance in the streets twenty-four hours at a stretch. After the celebrations King Audie retired to his office down beside the back steps and relaxed on his mat. The office has a covering of canvas and used to be the woodshed until the king took over. He keeps his treasures there. He has a small table, a chair, a mat, some drinking-straws, two match-boxes, some woollen wigs made out of balls of wool in his spare time, and several half-used rolls of coloured toilet paper snatched from the bathroom when I wasn't looking.

On David's sixth birthday I gave him a small party. I had never attempted this before, but the previous year, at Ellen's party, I had noticed him hanging round the guests, and although he hid from time to time, it was obvious that he found the whole affair attractive—particularly the cake, which at one stage he tried to stand on. So for his party I made him a cake for himself.

He sat on his father's lap while we lit the candles and sang "Happy Birthday". Looking pleased, he leant forward and blew out the candles. We all started laughing and talking at once. David seemed quite proud of himself. He took his father's hand, placed it on the matchbox, and guided it to-wards the cake. My husband lit the candles again. David blew them out again, then indicated that he wanted them lit again. When I tried to cut the cake he fought me. His father had to go on lighting the candles over and over. When my husband tired of this, I took over, and when I gave up Roley had to carry on. It was quite a day. He wouldn't let anybody eat the cake, but he enjoyed his party.

David is becoming more confident in himself as time goes by. In the past we watched him cry his lonely way through hours of depression when, as he became more aware of his environ-ment, some glimpse of reality proved too much for his im-mature nervous system to bear. We watched his anguish as he hid his face in fear and cried at some emotional hurt too subtle for us to detect. We were helpless to soothe him be-cause he was unable to seek comfort from us and had to bear his distress in isolation. Over the years we have watched him develop from a frightened little boy into a confident though extremely limited one. His confidence does not always extend beyond his own environment into others, but he is improving surely.

Toilet training is still a big problem. I have managed to persuade him to urinate into a receptacle, but he doesn't know the difference between one receptacle and another. This poses problems when I take him out visiting. He will urinate into anything that attracts his attention. Afternoon tea parties are out.

An added difficulty is that often—possibly because of tension—he can't urinate at all and will cry with the discomfort of a full bladder that he can't empty. At such times he has to become absorbed in something else before he can find relief. This problem comes and goes at different levels of intensity, but he never quite gains control. Tests of his urine have revealed nothing abnormal.

Socially he is still all at sea. Even if he ever does learn to speak fluently—which seems unlikely now—he will still have a certain awkwardness that he will probably never be able to overcome.

Ellen once called him a "social blot", and it is true that he is very hard to explain to people who have never heard of his condition. Some distant relatives once called on us unexpectedly, and went away shortly afterwards dumbfounded, shaking chops from the soles of their shoes and Gran Bits from their pockets. On one of his really active days David could be replaced by an earthquake and you wouldn't know the difference.

We have now begun to discipline him. We introduce only one rule at a time, letting him absorb one restriction before starting on another. Once we've made a rule we can never go back on it, so we have to limit ourselves to the necessary ones. We must be consistent.

He now understands that he must go to bed at 9.30 and stay there all night. It makes no sense to him, but he knows that if he doesn't do it he will meet with our disapproval. We showed our disapproval by giving him a slap, waiting till he was aware of the reason for the slap. I have never slapped him while he was under stress. When he was hysterical and lashing out blindly in panic I sometimes got in the way of his flailing limbs, but I didn't hit him back; I don't think he would have known what it was for. I tried not to lose my head and behave the way he did. I did my best to behave the way I wanted him to behave. Nowadays he stays in bed till the lunches are cut in the morning. This is a wonderful improvement. We had to wait till David had recovered from his autistic state to do this. While he was withdrawn we could do very little with him.

The fact that David has recovered from his autistic state does not mean that he is no longer handicapped. He is no longer in such a sleepwalking state, he is now more aware of his environment, but he still doesn't understand the world or what use to make of things. Sometimes his brain seems to be like a telephone switchboard that keeps getting crossed lines. For example, I said to a friend, "David is a good boy now, he doesn't eat sand any more." David looked pleased with himself at the praise, ran outside, and came back with his mouth full of sand, smiling proudly.

His sense of his own identity is still not clear. Just because he can see other people doesn't necessarily mean that he knows he is the same and can do the same things. He is beginning to copy, but still in a baby way. Sometimes he tries to copy his father. David always sits in the same armchair to read his paper and places his feet on a foot-rest. Little David often sits in a corresponding armchair, after dragging another foot-rest into position for his feet. Sometimes little David takes the phone book out to place in front of a veranda chair to rest his feet on.

David's asthma has now disappeared and his health has greatly improved. Sometimes his rash reappears and we have a few days of grumbling and ointment. On the whole, however, his skin is fairly healthy and in warm weather he spends most of his time in the sun.

It is almost as though David's bones and muscles, his frame, developed normally till the time of birth, but that his nervous system, digestive system, and skin developed at a slower rate, so that when he was born he was partly at the premature stage. He had to cope with the outside world before he could tolerate it. Perhaps the trauma of being born was too much for David. I sometimes wonder, too, whether the shock of circumcision was more than he could stand.

He is learning to be patient. Whereas once he would scream and throw himself to the floor if I didn't pour out his fruit juice in three seconds flat when he was thirsty, he now merely holds onto my dress and waits, his mug in hand, till I can put away whatever I am working on and get to the refrigerator. He is learning to stand in line with other members of the family. He is beginning to realize that he is not alone, that he is part of a unit, that we want him and like to be with him, but that he must take others into account. This is very hard for him to learn.

Sometimes when he has hurt himself he runs away and sits alone and kicks at anybody who tries to comfort him, but more often he lets us pat and comfort him.

These days he laughs more than he cries. He rarely throws a tantrum.

I once had a strange dream about him. I dreamt I saw the fear step away from his body and stand alone, like a shadow of himself. His own body stood stiff and silent like a wooden doll, and I stepped into the shape of the fear. I became one with the fear, his sensitive self; I felt as he does and saw with his eyes. I saw human beings through one eye in the forehead of the fear; I saw a narrow vision of the world. And through one ear I heard disjointed sounds coming and going. I saw a world peopled with strange moving shapes, human beings, shapes that didn't stay in one place but kept moving out of my range of vision. And just when I got adjusted to them standing in one place for a little while and assessed them against one background, they moved, and flickered back and forth like reflections in a stream when the surface of the water is disturbed. I heard the voices of human beings—strange chattering noises coming out of holes in their heads, distorted heads. They never said the same thing twice in the same way. Every time the words came out they sounded different, of a different pitch. Sometimes there was a blackness, a nothing all around me, and I felt afraid, and I reached out and clung to something solid, a piece of furniture that stayed in one place. Then I heard music and was comforted. I liked the music because it followed recognizable patterns and I knew what to expect of it. Then I heard a voice saying, "You are a nothing." And I tried to answer, but I couldn't speak; I could only think, and I thought, "I am not a nothing. I don't know what I am, but I can feel and think, so I am not a nothing. I am just different."

After I had had this dream I thought a lot about autistic children. I thought about all the faces I had seen, faces with busy expressions, quiet expressions, sad expressions, and some with no expressions at all, and I felt pity. When I saw these children struggling and fighting and kicking in their moments of frustration I understood how they felt. These are the children who walk in the shadows, and the road they walk is lonely and empty. They don't know how to take advantage of the warmth of human company. If a child can't find safety in his mother's arms, where else can he find it? How can a child develop into a human being if he doesn't know how to make contact with human beings?

When David was very young I resigned myself to the fact that he was severely handicapped, and at one stage I really thought that he would never improve. But he is far more aware now than I ever hoped he would be. He continues to show signs of wanting to join in family activities. Last Guy Fawkes night he came outside with us to watch the fireworks and sat on the steps spellbound. Even though he ran and hid on all fours behind a tree when the rockets were fired, he obviously enjoyed the experience.

He no longer runs out into oncoming traffic without any idea that he is in danger, but draws back from fast-moving cars in a normal response to danger. Only a year ago he would stand in the path of the motor-mower when the lawn was being cut, oblivious of its roar, not knowing that he should get out of its way. Now he gets out of its path as soon as he hears it.

Occasionally I realize how much he has progressed when I talk to another mother of an autistic child. Richard's mother phoned recently to say that she was worried by his habit of turning on the electric stove while he was sitting on the hotplate. David used to do the same thing, but grew out of it fairly quickly. I had forgotten about this till Jane phoned.

Living with an autistic child for six years has taught me to take each day as it comes. I have learned that there are many levels of sorrow and that I can't stay at the deepest level for long. Life goes on and I must join in. I try not to worry about the future. I can't live all my life at once. Just one day at a time. I was forty when David was born and I think he will outlive me. This I hate to think about. What will happen to him when I die? To me my child is precious, and I know how much he needs my support. I love him because he is part of me, but I have to face the fact that he may never say another word.

As I said earlier, I've been helped over a lot of David's difficult phases by the knowledge that each one was only a phase and would pass. When I first saw him repeatedly doing something intolerable I was inclined to despair and wonder how I would manage him when he was twenty if he continued this way. Then I grew to realize that in time he would drop this activity and pass on to something else. The new activity often brought fresh problems, but I knew that it, too, would pass and this made it easier for me. I have allowed David to go through his phases without too much interference. I have tried not to rush him. If he turned to me I offered support; for the rest, I let him have his head. If he became interested in some forbidden substance I provided him with substitutes whenever possible. When he ate Ellen's Plasticine I provided him with flour-and-water dough. When he wanted to eat stones I gave him Gran Bits. And so on. If he showed interest in some pursuit I allowed him to follow it as much as I could. Some people might regard his collecting of toilet paper as a waste of money, but, since he has no interest in normal toys, toilet paper is not extravagant. Most children have a certain amount of money spent on toys. David's toy money is spent on other things.

His nature at present reminds me of a cat's. He sits where it is comfortable, without reasoning beyond his own comfort. He lies naked on the warm cement in the sun or finds a patch of sun under a window and curls up there. If he sits on your lap he expects you to support him in the position that suits him. It doesn't occur to him that you might overbalance.

Now that he is showing more awareness of people and noises, he sometimes covers his eyes when he hears a loud noise, or his ears when he sees something new. He's not sure whether he hears with his ears or his eyes, or whether he sees with his eyes or his ears.

He is interested in babies when somebody is holding them and often tries to crawl into a baby's pram, but he is distressed by toddlers. Anything moving about out of his control and below his eye level causes him uneasiness.

I have been most fortunate in having the kind of husband I have. Little David could never have developed to his present stage of accepting people if his father had not been so good to him. Big David never wavers in his loyalty and support. And besides being a most consistent person he is also, of course, a trained psychologist.

When David and I first married I had hoped that when my children started school I'd be able to get some organization going to aid prisoners' families. I do visit these families, but not on the scale I had hoped. There are many agencies doing fine work of this sort, but I had hoped to start one devoted solely to promoting research and providing opportunities, and even scholarships, for the children of prisoners. I have a lot of ideas that I have not yet been able to put into practice, but I expect to achieve my aims in time.

In the course of my many visits to parents of autistic children I've never ceased to wonder at the resourcefulness I've seen. Some mothers give expert care to their normal children as well as their autistic one, at the same time managing careers as well. One woman has autistic twin girls as well as a young family of normal children. Another has one autistic child, one retarded child, and one normal child.

I've often wondered about Dr Leo Kanner's theory (mentioned in Chapter 3) that the majority of parents of autistic children are "refrigerator people"—humourless, obsessional, rational people who dislike frivolity. I don't know if all the affected children I have met are really autistic, though they seem to me to fit the descriptions of autism I have read in books. Their parents, however, certainly don't fit Dr Kanner's description. As a group, they impress me as being slightly above average in intelligence, and many are quite talented. They are very emotional people who appear to love their autistic children and to be deeply moved by the children's distress.

But, of course, I have met only a very small sample.

Many people think that all sorts of magical things can be done in mental institutions, and I'm often asked why I don't put David into one.

There was a time when most afflicted children could be institutionalized. If a doctor noticed anything amiss at birth or early in the child's life he often advised the parents to put the child into an institution and have another one to take its place. This certainly spared parents who were trying to rear normal children. But I think that doctors take a risk if they tell parents that there is little likelihood of their producing a second handicapped child. I know one mother who produced four handicapped children in a row. She claims that she was assured each time that there was little chance it would happen again. Over the last few years I have met so many children with handicaps of which the causes are not fully understood.

Now that the solution of placing a handicapped child in an institution is no longer so readily available, many mothers tell me they are wondering whether they should have any more children. Some mothers have broken down under the strain of living with their difficult children and have themselves been forced to enter mental hospitals.

Victoria's Mental Health Authority has a waiting-list of over 1600 at present and this number is increasing at the rate of about 100 a year. This number, of course, includes all those who are mentally handicapped, not only the few autistic children. There are also waiting-lists for private institutions.

Actually, the waiting-list is not only due to the increase in population. It is also due partly to the fact that conditions have improved considerably over the last few years. More parents are able to face the prospect of having their children placed when conditions are good. And this improvement in conditions has been brought about in no small measure by the work of parents themselves. They formed committees and fought for better conditions and less overcrowding for their handicapped children. Mrs Ethel Temby, who is vice-president of Kew Cottages and St Nicholas Parents' Associations, told me how over the years she and her fellow-members have written hundreds of letters to members of parliament, given endless public talks to interested groups, and written articles for the press. One parent, June Epstein, has even written a book on the problems of the mentally handicapped, *Image of the King: A Parent's Story of Mentally Handicapped Children*, published by Ure Smith.

Mental Health Authority recently established a new centre that will cater for children who are psychiatrically ill, including autistic children. There are out-patient and in-patient facilities, and fully integrated diagnostic and therapeutic programmes employing both physical and psychotherapeutic techniques. Treatment is free. Already this one section has a waiting-list of thirty children. It should provide excellent opportunities for research.

In talking to parents of autistic children I have discovered many different attitudes towards the treatment services provided by the State of Victoria. At first I couldn't understand why some parents spoke highly of these services and others complained bitterly. So far as I could learn, all children had equal opportunities for being assessed by well-trained people in the Education Department, Mental Health Authority or the Children's Hospital. While Victoria had never had a centre designed solely to cater for autistic children, it was possible to have them placed in various types of day centres and schools along with other slow-learning and mentally handicapped children. Some parents I spoke to had sent their children to normal kindergartens and on to primary schools, and most of these seemed well satisfied with the work of the teachers. Other parents had children who were assessed as suitable for special schools for slow learners or other schools for handicapped children. Some of these children had eventually passed on to normal schools. Their parents had no specific complaints about the assessment or teachers. Occasionally I spoke to parents who were disappointed with the progress their child had made, but they did not blame the teachers; they simply thought their child was too handicapped to get on.

Now and then I met parents whose children had been classified as all but ineducable and in need of full-time institutional care. I know of five children with autistic symptoms whose parents have placed them in institutions full-time in the belief that they were incapable of making enough progress to continue being cared for at home. These parents were more than relieved to have their children settled and would not consider bringing them home again permanently and sending them to day centres. Three of the children are in Mental Health institutions and two in private centres.

Parents dissatisfied with treatment services in Victoria were, in the main, those whose children had been classified as unsuitable for existing day centres. Most of these children had little or no speech and registered poorly in tests or had been considered too disturbed to benefit from available services. Their parents often believed them capable of better performances than the official assessment indicated. Autistic children are notorious for registering poorly in intelligence tests and the like. They don't seem to try. But many parents still prefer to keep their autistic children at home and send them to day centres rather than place them in residential care. Parents of autistic children who can speak have recently been giving thought to putting them in centres devoted to autistic children instead of other types of day centres and normal schools.

For instance, one mother whose autistic son had been accepted as a pupil at a State school for normal children decided to remove him and pay for his tuition at a very good private school for handicapped children. She says she could ill afford it, but couldn't stand seeing her son so miserable. He was capable of learning with normal children, but was slow and nervous and couldn't stand up to the teasing of the other children. His sense of failure was so great that his mother thought it more sensible to place him among slow learners where he could shine as a clever pupil.

I think that the community could do with more half-way help for parents. Mental Health Authority provides complete relief in that the child is boarded away from the family, or it provides out-patient treatment. But we need a place to leave autistic children while the mother shops or visits the dentist or calls on friends. Baby-minding centres are not geared for autistic children, and baby-sitters are usually totally unprepared for what is in store for them when they undertake to sit with one. It is not fair to the child or to the sitter if the sitter has no understanding of the condition. In my own experience, sitters come in three types. The first type is most

K

sympathetic and sincerely wants to help, but finds the task too demanding. The second type decides to "train" the child during the parents' absence. She feels that all the child needs is a bit of straightening out, and she undertakes to do in an hour what nobody else has been able to do in years. She could do a lot of damage. The third type is rare. She listens to what the parent has to say about the condition and does as she is asked. She offers the child support if he looks for it, but doesn't try to force him to do anything that is beyond him. It is hardly fair to expect a stranger to grasp the problems in a short space of time, but some sitters are able to understand enough to coast along till the mother's return.

I always dread leaving David with a sitter; I never know what to expect when I return. I have a few friends who are marvellous with him, but he is hard work for the general run of sitters, and I rarely go out unless I really need to.

When David was a baby I had the feeling that everything was closing in on me, that no matter where I turned there was no help. In fact, nobody offered help then because nobody realized that I had a problem. Once David's condition became apparent to other people I got many offers of help.

Mrs Elizabeth Mirfield has become interested in helping me with David and she sometimes drops in for an hour or so while I have a sleep through the afternoon. She keeps an eye on David and he is getting to know her. Two other girls who have offered to help out in emergencies are Jan Dear and Peggy Stirling. They have family responsibilities of their own but can usually help out when I am desperate.

With the long waiting-lists for the established institutions, the need for day centres where autistic children can be minded by the hour or by the day is obvious. But I believe that care should be taken in the setting up of such centres. Money for equipment is necessary, of course, but autistic children don't need a great deal of equipment. What they need most is highly qualified staff to care for them. I have already discussed, in Chapter 5, the centres established by the Victorian Autistic Children's Association.

Some people are most optimistic about teaching autistic children, even those who can't speak, and, as we have seen, there are many theories about how they should be handled.

A child psychiatrist recently told me that all teaching methods at present being applied are still hypothetical, even though there have been some successes with some children. Nobody, he said, is really getting down to the heart of the problem, which is research.

One very active parent of an autistic child is Dr Joan Curtis. She has written a booklet on the care of the autistic child at home, made an educational film called *Autism Without Tears*, and, as well, practises as a specialist obstetrician in a Victorian country town. She has two sons, a seven-year-old who is normal and a four-year-old who is autistic. Her husband is also a doctor.

Not long ago she spoke to several Apex Club groups, and aroused their interest in autism. This interest eventually spread to the federal convention in Sydney, and some time later we were informed that the money raised from a planned "Walkathon" around Australia would be donated for research into autism. The walkers set out from Adelaide, South Australia, in March 1969 and travelled clockwise round Australia, following Highway 1 and passing through all States. They completed the venture in November 1969, returning to Adelaide about $120,000 richer. This money has been set up in a trust fund.

Dr Curtis has also written to the *Australian Medical Journal* outlining the symptoms of autism and stressing the need for early diagnosis.

The help that a minding centre can give mothers of handicapped children is something I can now describe from my own experience, thanks to Mrs Dowell. I have known Mrs Dowell for only a short time. She is married to a doctor and has a son who was a victim of encephalitis during babyhood. The need for minding facilities for handicapped children was realized by Mrs Dowell through her own difficulties. After her son was accepted as a three-day-a-week pupil at a day centre, Mrs Dowell, with a group of her friends, decided to open a minding centre at Donvale, a Melbourne suburb. They formed a committee and obtained the free use of the Donvale Recreation Centre two days a week. They work to a roster, with one trained nurse on duty with each group, but make no claims about training handicapped children. They simply mind each child according to the mother's instructions. They raise their own funds and so far have managed to provide each child with something to interest it. They have mattresses for the children's rest periods, special chairs and strollers for those who can't walk, and lots of toys and balloons for those who like them.

David now attends this centre two days a week. A full programme at a training centre, lasting almost a full school day, is beyond David for the time being, with his bladder and bowel difficulties, but the minding centre gives him some experience of coping with new people and allows him to gain some confidence by entering a new environment for short periods without my presence.

For some time I have wondered about the wisdom of placing David in a centre peopled with autistic children only. David is passing through a very gentle stage, and many autistic children undergoing teaching programmes are very aggressive and scream a lot; they are also frequently antisocial. David is beginning to form shaky human relationships, and to place him in the midst of a group of children who would not welcome him could set him back. David will eventually attend a centre for autistic children, but the Donvale Centre is breaking him in gently. It is rather like a kindergarten for slow-thinking children. They have play equipment but no firm routine, apart from morning and afternoon walks and meal and drink times. While the children attending are mostly severely handicapped in many different ways, none of them, as far as I can see, is antisocial. They are willing to make friends if they are capable of knowing someone is there. If they can move their arms they hold them out to people. Some of these children are very affectionate. One small boy with mongolism follows David around trying to make friends. One day I saw him running behind David, hanging on to David's shirt, and they were both laughing. Another time he tried to play peek-a-boo with David round the door. These attempts at friendliness make some impression on David; even though he sometimes turns his back, he smiles to himself when an advance is made.

So far he has not copied any of the other children's handicaps. If he spent much time with children who couldn't walk

I think he might begin to copy them, but while some of the children in this centre can't walk, some can, and in any case David is there for only a small proportion of his time.

Children come and go at the centre. Some spend a little time there while waiting to be placed in residential institutions, some are absent for a while when they have to go into hospital for tests to be carried out. But I think this type of public service is invaluable, and so do the other mothers. No charge is made and no mother is asked to raise funds or serve on the committee. The children are picked up by voluntary drivers and brought home at about three o'clock. That gives the mother time to shop and collect her wits.

Mrs Dowell is certain that the need exists for her type of minding centre and hopes for more recognition of this need. She also hopes for more suitable surroundings for the children and helpers some day. She would like to obtain a government subsidy instead of existing on charity; she thinks that handicapped children are all entitled to their share of government funds as are normal children who are educated free. This is David's third week at this new centre, and it has made things a lot easier for me. I can now keep appointments two days a week, and, as one mother said, it makes you feel more like other people.

I I

THIS LAST WINTER HAS BEEN A LONG ONE FOR ME. DAVID HAS been aware of all the fun he has missed by not being allowed to play outside in the cold rain. He is becoming more aware of heat and cold and although he wants to play outside and sit in the water he cries when he gets wet because it is cold. This frustrates him.

This year the council began to seal the roads and install drains in our suburb. The backyard fences along our street were removed to allow earth-moving equipment to pass through, and deep drains were dug the full length of our block. The makeshift drains of the past were ploughed up and drain water ran all over the place. At one stage, every time bath water was released in our house a neighbour's swimming-pool filled. Everybody complained about everybody else's drain water.

Little David realized he had struck a bonanza. He had never known so much wonderful mucky water. Every time he got outside he made straight for the drains. He walked in mud up to his knees, ran into neighbours' yards, and foraged round in their garages for unspeakable liquids to drink. Whenever I lost sight of him I knew he would be found lying full-length in some open drain, on his back, with only his mouth and nose exposed. From this position he could disappear altogether and blow a huge fountain of muddy water into the air through his mouth. He discovered to his delight that he could wander the whole length of the street without getting out of the drains.

I almost gave up the idea of writing. Twenty minutes at the typewriter was a luxury. Every time David escaped I had to race out into the rain and drag him back, screaming and fighting, covered in mud from head to foot.

I kept phoning the council and asking them to put up the fences. They were sympathetic but helpless. The drain project had to continue, David or no David. I warned all the tractor men to watch out for him and told them he was deaf and couldn't hear the machines coming. That was the easiest way of describing him.

The more alert David becomes, the harder he is to look after. Each new accomplishment he acquires he puts to some fiendish use, often chuckling as he makes some new discovery. One day, for instance, I found him laughing softly to himself as he hid his rissoles in Ellen's new boudoir slippers.

This year he took up typing. Whenever I left an un-finished page in my machine I returned to find a row of question marks and Double Holland words typed across it. Once he held me up for some time by tipping a small jar of honey into the typewriter. Another time he flushed ten thousand words of copy down the toilet. I did get three articles written during the year, but don't know how I did it.

David's compulsion to explore is a sign that he is coming out of his lost state, that he is no longer autistic. He is obviously damaged from his years of isolation and he still has a severe communication problem, but he is reaching out more and more. Some days he looks so alert he gives the impression of a keen, waiting intelligence ready to be released. He still does some astonishingly silly things, but he also does some reason-able things. And he is trying. There is a natural development. I am sure his eyes and ears are picking up more. I am sure, for example, that he can now separate figures from back-grounds. When he wants my hand to do something for him he never mistakes the chair for my hand now. He also knows by sight the clothes I am wearing. For instance, he knows that if he grabs my skirt I come with it and he can see my arm against a cushion. He knows that I am a whole thing, joined together. He no longer feels for my hand, he goes straight to it without hesitation. This is a sign that he is aware of my shape against backgrounds. I sometimes wonder whether his distorted vision was at all akin to colour-blindness.

He now understands a lot of conversation. On Saturday and Sunday mornings Ellen sits on his bed and tells him, "It's a Daddy day today." And he jumps up and down with glee, and throws his pillow all over the room with excitement. Then he keeps looking at the door, waiting for his father to come in and play with him.

He is lucky to have such an understanding big sister. All through the years when he ignored her she kept trying to contact him and interest him. Now he romps with her and they run up and down the hall playing chasing games. He is still clumsy and sometimes bumps into her, but he laughs when he sees her running towards him. She calls him "the boy with the wild brain", or "nature boy", or "King Audie of Double Holland". She goes to endless trouble to cultivate him. She is patient and good-natured, and really loves him. I can only hope that having had to adapt herself to living with a mentally ill child has not made her too different from other children.

Roley has not adjusted to little David as well as Ellen. I don't thing he will ever be able to relax completely with a handicapped child in the house. He feels pity, but can't help his sense of discomfort. He is much more accepting than he used to be, however, and he often laughs at David's funny antics. David doesn't seem to know the difference between his hands and his feet and sometimes wears gloves on his feet. This amuses Roley. He also laughs when David wears the crust of a loaf of bread on his ankle. The baker took to handing the bread to David at the front gate. David would eat out the middle and then slip his foot through the crust.

We have had to call the police twice in the last year when David went for a walk without our knowledge. Once he disappeared when a friend was minding him. She found him at the nearest police station where he was giving the policeman on duty a good run for his money. The policeman said he found him a handful. The second time he got up early one morning and went for a walk while we were all asleep. He was missing for about an hour and we had to call the local police to help search.

Having to describe David to a stranger over the phone is not easy at seven o'clock in the morning, before you have had time to collect your wits. I told the policeman that David was autistic, but he seemed not to know what I was talking about, so I said he was retarded. Then I had to describe his appearance. Six years old, either wearing his sister's nightie or naked; hops instead of walking; his name is David, but he doesn't come when you call, "David", only when you call, "Car, car". His hair is fairly long and probably very untidy.

David had rifled the bread tin before taking off and I didn't know whether to say that he could have been wearing a crust of bread on his ankle or not. My rubber gloves were also missing, so I could have added, "may be wearing rubber gloves on his feet", but I didn't. I had given the policeman enough to go on with and he had to broadcast the description over the radio. I felt I had already gone far enough. If I had given a full description someone would probably have thought it was a hoax. Who would believe such a child existed? As Roley says, you don't have to be mad to have an autistic child in the family, but it helps.

Each time I see changes in little David I feel a lightness in my heart. Given his early state of almost complete non-communication, any progress is welcome, any change exciting. With each new happening I feel a fresh stirring of hope.

I feel that there must be many children born with slight brain damage, milder than David's, who never learn to communicate fully. There must be many people who live out their lives capable only of limited communication; outwardly they would seem normal, but their human relationships must suffer. If David's type of damage doesn't show up in any known tests, then milder types of damage would have even less chance of showing up. Surely certain children whose mothers find them difficult to teach could be suffering from mild brain damage. So many things can go wrong during a pregnancy or confinement. A mild infection suffered by a pregnant woman could have lasting affects on the behaviour of the child. I have been taking thyroid tablets ever since

David's birth, and I feel quite well while I take them. I often wonder whether my thyroid imbalance could have contributed to David's condition.

This year I planted six daffodil bulbs in the back garden, and one came up. Usually everything I plant dies, but this one daffodil flourished. It was a distinguished-looking flower with a long slender stem, and one daffodil is as good as six if you like it enough. And little David liked this daffodil. He knew that something flourished where there had previously been nothing. He got down on his hands and knees to study it every day. Sometimes he turned his head sideways to get a better look at it, and waved his hand back and forth in front of it.

One morning I was hanging the washing on the line, and at the same time keeping an eye on David. There were dewdrops on the daffodil, and as they sparkled in the sun David touched them and smiled. I finished hanging up the last garment and took a deep breath of fresh clean air. In the distance the mist was rising from the Dandenong Mountains and they stood out deep blue along the horizon. It was two days before spring, and although there was not much heat in the sun the prospect of summer warmth cheered me. Soon David would be able to play outside all day every day—the fences had been replaced, much to my relief—and the washing would dry on the line in a few hours instead of drooping forlornly all over the house for weeks. We had lived through another winter of David's uneasy wailing at being shut inside the house when all the lovely rain was going to waste outside. Another winter of childhood ailments and doctors' bills was behind us.

I called David. He ignored me. I called again. He waddled towards me, walking sideways like a crab. He grinned and looked at the ground self-consciously. He was showing off.

I bent down to talk to him and he reached up, put his hands round my neck, and kissed me clumsily on the cheek. Then he backed away sheepishly. He had never kissed anyone before.

We walked over to the back steps together and sat down. We looked up at the treetops stirring in the breeze. The back

146

steps are David's favourite place, and he likes to watch the changing shapes of trees moving against the sky. When I put my arm round him he looked at me curiously and dabbed his finger in the tear trickling down my cheek. His eyes were thoughtful. There was nothing blank about his expression now. He leant his head against my shoulder.

I think little David would like to join the world of people. If only he can find the way.

BOOKS ABOUT AUTISM

I DON'T WANT TO GIVE A LIST OF RECOMMENDED READING material on autism, because that might give the impression that I was in agreement with all the views expressed in each book. Nobody can be in agreement with all the views expressed in any half-dozen books on autism, because the people who write them aren't in agreement. Sometimes they write about different groups of children. Obviously they have not all studied the same children; they have studied children who resemble each other in some aspects of their behaviour.

Doctor Bruno Bettelheim's *The Empty Fortress* (The Free Press, 1967) I found interesting for the descriptions of the children and the methods of handling them. But I don't go along with the concept that the children behaved as they did because of the environment. While Doctor Bettelheim's success rate in the handling of disturbed children is remarkably high, he is not very popular with parents I have spoken to. The children, however, must learn to love him; he certainly leaves no stone unturned to give them a trouble-free existence. I should be quite happy to let Doctor Bettelheim handle David.

Doctor Bettelheim, who I believe studied under Freud, is principal of Chicago University's Sonia Shankman Orthogenic School for Psychotic Children. It is perhaps indicative of Doctor Bettelheim's ingenuity that he is able to convince parents that they have contributed to their children's illnesses while charging them $8000 a year for the privilege. The school is said to be one of the best-staffed anywhere in the world, with hot and cold running therapists available twenty-four hours a day. It actually costs around $12,000 a year for each pupil, but the difference is made up of foundation grants and donations by grateful parents.

Doctor Gerald O'Gorman, in *The Nature of Childhood Autism* (Butterworth, 1967), covers a wide range of children with symptoms of an autistic type and gives a view of how they differ in aetiology. Doctor O'Gorman is Physician Superintendent at Borocourt Hospital, Reading, Berkshire.

The proceedings of a conference on the autistic child held in Adelaide, South Australia, in August 1967 were published under the title *Autism, Cure Tomorrow, Care Today*. This book contains many interesting opinions and can be purchased by writing to the Autistic Children's Association of South Australia, 1 Launceston Avenue, Warradale, South Australia. The cost is $2 plus postage.

There is a pamphlet-type book, *Autistic Children*, written for the guidance of parents who have an autistic child and wish to know what this might mean and what steps they can take to minimize their child's handicaps. Although the services it mentions are those available in England and don't apply to Australia, this is a most enlightening and helpful book. I think it covers most aspects of autism without going into long explanations. It is published by the National Association for Mental Health in co-operation with the National Society for Autistic Children, 39 Queen Anne Street, London W1. The author is Doctor Lorna Wing of Maudsley Hospital, London.

A second booklet by Doctor Lorna Wing, *Children Apart: Autistic Children and Their Families*, published by the British Medical Association in conjunction with the National Association for Mental Health, is similar to the other booklet, but I think the second one is even clearer for the layman.

After reading *Early Childhood Autism: Clinical, Educational and Social Aspects*, published by Pergamon Press in 1966 and edited by Doctor J. K. Wing, I felt that there could hardly be anything left for anyone else to say. This book covered so many angles and gave so many opinions and theories.

Doctor Bernard Rimland's *Infantile Autism*, published in 1965 by Methuen, London, is one of the best books I have read so far.

Australian Associations

Autistic Children's Association of New South Wales.
Secretary, Mrs Margaret Vern-Barnett, P.O. Box 18, Chatswood, N.S.W. 2067.

Victorian Autistic Children's Association.
Secretary, Mrs Cusack, St Andrew's Church Hall, 580 Balcombe Road, Black Rock, Victoria 3193.

Association for Autistic Children, Western Australia.
Secretary, Mr D. Haines, 101 Milne Street, Bayswater, W.A. 6053.

Autistic Children's Association of Queensland.
Secretary, Mr S. D. Nelson, 4 Inville Street, Geebung, Queensland 4053.

Autistic Children's Association of South Australia.
Secretary, Mr Peter Tillett, 1 Launceston Avenue, Warradale, S.A. 5046.

Autistic Children's Association of Tasmania.
Secretary, Mrs F. Craske, 65 Derwent Avenue, Lindisfarne, Tasmania 7015.

National Associations

The National Society for Autistic Children.
100 Wise Lane, Mill Hill, London N.W.7, United Kingdom.

The National Society for Autistic Children.
6200 29th Street, North West, Washington D.C. 20015, U.S.A.

New Zealand Autistic Children's Association.
Liaison Officer, Mrs Marion Bruce, 11 Amarua Street, Elsdon, New Zealand.

South Africa: Transvaal Society for Autistic Children.
Chairman, Mr J. Kahan, 6 Kyhrin Street, Rouxville, Johannesburg.